CRIME INVESTIGATED

IAN BRADY and MYRA HINDLEY

MURDER ON THE MOORS

igloobooks

igloobooks

Published in 2014
by Igloo Books Ltd
Cottage Farm
Sywell
NN6 0BJ
www.igloobooks.com

Project managed by HL Studios

HUN001 0214
2 4 6 8 10 9 7 5 3 1
ISBN 978-1-78343-120-5

Printed and manufactured in China

Contents

Ian Brady
and
Myra Hindley

Introduction

Brady and Hindley both worked at Millwards Merchandising, where they first met and dated. This book explores their working life and their early courtship, including the characteristics of their personalities. It looks at why they were attracted to each other and how, over time, their relationship gradually became more dependent on each other, and their sexual relationship became more sinister, extreme and bizarre.

The murders are detailed within this book, as well as the lengths Brady and Hindley went through to conceal their crimes whilst keeping a sick coded trophy enshrining the memory of the event, such as the seemingly normal photograph of Myra Hindley posing with her dog on Saddleworth Moors. The fact that this seemingly nonchalant tourist attraction snap, contained a secret code was not known until nearly thirty years later. This photograph was later revealed to be the location of the child victim, John Kilbride.

When reading books about serial killers it is all too easy to immerse yourself in the salacious details surrounding the gruesome facts and lose yourself in the story. However fascinating in an un-worldly way, it should be remembered that the events described, the brutality of the killings and the morbid horror and pain that would have been felt by the victims is no fictional event. These people were real human beings, although this term could only be biologically correct when applied to the perpetrators of these heinous crimes, and the events described are real life events.

This should never be forgotten when reading through the events of serial killers and partners, Ian Brady and Myra Hindley. The crimes of this couple were not just barbaric murders, but were also sinister through the sexualisation and torture of their victims. When reading the description of each murder, remember that the majority of their victims were innocent, defenceless children whose last living memory on this earth would have been of bewilderment, that their torturers were two adults. Children were told in this era, *'If in danger find an adult'*, and maternal nature gave children the instinct that adult women were to be trusted more than adult men. Yet it is more shocking, as the horrific fatal pain was inflicted upon their tiny bodies, that their innocent child eyes would have lain upon those of a man and woman who were clearly enjoying their sadistic acts as a couple. Even though a child may not have conscious philosophical thoughts, it must be true that the subconscious cortex of their brain would have been trying to compute and desperately find, through basic human and Darwinian instinct, a way of survival from the situation. It is the reason these murders were so inhumane that the last moments of these poor children would have been their looking into the eyes of an adult male and finding no paternal flickers, although perhaps more wrenching and shocking would have been looking into those of the woman. Words cannot express the absolute disbelief that despite how innocent and wretched their final pleas for survival were, the woman's eyes that looked back at them as they died, would have shown no trace of maternal caring or protection. Whether religious or not, there are many other words that could be used when describing the adult female and male perpetrators of this vile act, yet the one that is blunt but also has sufficient resonance is EVIL, and this is often used to describe the sinister, sadistic murders carried out by Ian Thomas

Brady and Myra Hindley. It is the belief of many that both these people personify the word EVIL, a fact that is hard for a normal person to disagree with.

This book also goes back in time before the murders and explores what is known about the early lives of Ian Brady and Myra Hindley. It is unfortunate that other true details may be irretrievably embedded in the memories of Brady and Hindley about circumstances that shaped their early life, and in particular those happy and traumatic events, which would help enable us to understand how they became the people they were. That information would serve to help the psychiatrists, sociologists, criminologists and psychologists of today to decipher whether anything could be learned from Brady and Hindely's gradual decline from seemingly normal working-class folk, who worked from nine to five in middle management positions, into sadistic, paedophilic murderers.

Brady and Hindley both worked at Millwards Merchandising, where they first met and dated. This book explores their working life and their early courtship, including looking into the characteristics of their personalities. It investigates why they were attracted to each other and how, over time, their relationship gradually became more inter-dependent, and their sexual relationship became more sinister, extreme and bizarre.

The murders are detailed here, along with the lengths that Brady and Hindley went to, to conceal their crimes whilst keeping a sick coded trophy enshrining the memory of the event, such as the seemingly normal photograph of Myra Hindley posing with her pet dog on Saddleworth Moors. The fact that this otherwise nonchalant tourist attraction snap, contained a secret code, was not known until nearly thirty years later. This photograph was later revealed to have been taken at the location of the child victim, John Kilbride.

This book also goes through the arrest and investigation by the police, including a chapter on David Smith. Seventeen-year-old David Smith was the reason that Brady and Hindley were caught, because he informed Police of their crimes. He made a scared phone call from a public phone box with his partner, Maureen, the sister of Myra Hindley. David Smith was also a friend who grew close to Ian Brady. Their relationship became so close that Brady included him as a deliberate witness to him and Hindley in the murder of seventeen-year-old Edward Evans. Smith had been in the house when Edward was killed and was called in from the kitchen by his sister-in-law, Myra, to help when Brady was butchering Edward in the front room. David Smith watched as Edward Evans screamed just before Brady swung a hatchet into the left hand side of his already bloodied head. This section of the book explores the feelings of David Smith, his relationship with Brady and what he saw as their 'fantasist' conversations together over murder, and robbing banks.

In the present day, the life of Ian Thomas Brady continues in incarceration, although as detailed in the many letters he has sent in correspondence with various authors, media establishments and others, he is of the view that he is not a prisoner but rather a patient in a hospital receiving treatment. After the murders, and her subsequent trial and conviction, Myra Hyndley stayed in prison, and it was in prison that she suffered respiratory failure and allegedly died at Bury St Edmonds, West Suffolk Hospital, on the 16th November 2002. The word 'allegedly' is used, as in akin to her notoriety the events are somewhat unusual and create perfect fodder for conspiracy theorists. This book also explores the view that due to the impending Anderson report in December 2003 on 'life means life' for prisoners, which would have paved the way for Hindley's immediate release into public life, that her death was in fact staged and she has since been placed anonymously back into public life with protection. Whether or not one is reviled by this perhaps absurd conspiracy theory, British law is the way we keep morality enshrined in a democratic society and it is this that we must abide with if time ever reveals this theory to be fact.

It will be difficult whilst reading this book, not to gain some fascination with the actions of Brady and Hindley, to see it as another salacious story of a serial killer, made even more so by the fact that there were two killers, and that those two killers were in a sexual relationship together. It should not be forgotten, that Ian Thomas Brady and Myra Hindley were not just killers, but sadistic torturers as well. They took of this earth innocent lives and it is not just their victims who lost their young lives, it is also the families of the victims who continue to this day to suffer the loss. In the case of the victim Keith Bennett, whose body has never been found and is suspected to be buried somewhere on Saddleworth Moors. The pain that his mother, Winnie Johnson went though was a long-term torture as she tried to find the location of her young twelve-year-old son. Winnie died in 2012, and to date the grave has not been found. The way that so much pain, which doesn't diminish over time, could in a vile way provide a continuation of the sadistic pleasure, and reminder of his actions to the one living person who knows where the remains of the victims are. This person is Ian Thomas Brady.

The crimes of Ian Brady and Myra Hindley were not just barbaric murders, but the sexualisation and torture of their victims was also sinister, perhaps even evil. This fact should never be forgotten when reading through the history and events of the serial-killing couple's deranged life.

Chapter 1

The Troubled Child

The Troubled child

Forensic psychiatrists and FBI agents have tried to get inside the killer's mind. Traditional explanations include childhood abuse, genetics, chemical imbalances, brain injuries, exposure to traumatic events, and perceived societal injustices. The frightening implication is that a huge population has been exposed to one or more of these traumas. Is there some sort of lethal concoction that sets serial killers apart from the rest of the population?

Most people believe they have control over their impulses — no matter how angry they get, there is something that stops us from taking our aggression out on others. Theories abound that there are probably some moral safety latches lacking in serial killers, or that they are being controlled by something unfathomable.

Birth of a Sadist

Ian Brady was a bastard in the true sense of the word. Born on 2 January 1938 in the slums of Glasgow to tearoom waitress Margaret Stewart, Ian never met his father, or even knew who he was. As a child, he allegedly displayed chilling sadistic tendencies towards animals, including throwing a cat out of a window from the top floor of a high-rise building. These sickening qualities would later surface in adulthood, on his innocent victims.

As his mother was unable to cope, Ian was taken into foster care at only four months old, and raised by foster parents, John and Mary

Sloan. Although his mother frequently visited the foster home until he was twelve, she never revealed to the young Ian that she was his birth mother. Despite having a stable family life from such an early age, the young Ian was troubled, and his barbaric acts continued, such as setting a dog on fire for fun. His primary school, Camden Street, classed him as an underachiever and troublemaker who got into numerous fights with other children. Ian had a ferocious temper and would bang his head violently against a wall whenever he was angry. Neighbours described him as a 'terrible heartache' for his foster mother Mary, who tried in vain to bring up a stable child.

Explanation for his actions have been sought by alluding to a troubled childhood, yet Ian was provided with a loving and stable home from four months old. Through his life with John and Mary Sloan, he was nurtured and loved, but this did not stop his violent and sadistic character developing.

Nature Versus Nurture

It is easy to take the scant information about Ian's early childhood and neatly package it up into a Pandora's box of trouble waiting to happen. The recent findings of a 20-year research project carried out by the University of Pennsylvania, which set out to investigate the influence that 'normal' surroundings have on the development of the human brain, conclude that the experience of a stable, nurturing environment in early childhood is likely to increase the possibility of a better, society-accepted individual, regardless of genetics.

This research reinforces the widely accepted view that the 'parental role' is crucial in developing the cortex within the brain that best fits into human society, meaning a brain that is developed with cognitive, social, and emotional skills gained from an environment which is safe, normal, and full of a variety of human interaction.

On the surface, Ian's home life provided by John and Mary Sloan appears to have had all of these social ingredients. It is therefore easy to conclude that he must have been born 'bad', due to the appearance that the best possible 'nurture' was there from the beginning. Yet scratch the surface and a slightly different picture appears, one that gives more understanding of the fact that perhaps the surroundings in which the young Ian grew up might not have been conducive to positive childhood development, and could therefore provide an explanation as to the adult that Ian Brady became.

The 'stable' home in which Ian found himself was punctuated with Sunday visits from a nice lady called Peggy, as Margaret now liked to be known, who – when financially possible – provided him with gifts and clothes. For years in Ian's mind, Peggy was just a nice lady, and one can only imagine the impact it must have had on him when she was later revealed to be his biological mother. In addition, although not actually documented, the visits of Peggy, resplendent with goodies and the inevitable result of an animated Ian, must have had some influence on Mary Sloan. Mary was a kindly spirit who had answered an advertisement card left in a local newsagent window by Margaret, advertising her baby son for adoption. Perhaps Mary later regretted it, but when she met Margaret she agreed to take Ian. She sympathised with Margaret's plight, and agreed to allow regular contact with Ian anonymously. It would be only human to consider that Margaret had the easy option, her son financially taken care of, and without the hardship of discipline that parents have to endure, only being viewed by her son as the 'nice lady Peggy' who came every Sunday bearing gifts. Whether this had any ill effect on Mary Sloan, and if it did, whether or not those feelings were transferred to her treatment of Ian, we will never know.

One thing is sure, Ian felt like an outsider even within his family unit. This must have been difficult for him, as he was never legally adopted by the Sloans, and, though integrated within the family, Mary Sloan insisted that the young Ian call her 'Aunty', rather than 'Mum'. This isolation manifested itself at Camden Street Primary School where, instead of joining in with the other children's games, he would keep his distance and watch, standing perfectly still. This led to him being nicknamed 'Sloany' by his peers, a reference not only to his adopted surname, but also to his choice to remain separate and alone.

Influences

In his youth, he became fascinated with the The Third Reich and Hitler, and the atrocities committed by them. He was mesmerised by the Nazi pageantry and Nazi symbolism. He often asked other boys for souvenirs that their fathers brought back from the war, and when playing roughhouse war games, he would insist on being 'the German'. Some believe he likened Hitler to the 'father of the masses', and because Brady had no legitimate father, Hitler and his severe hatred for those unlike him, provided a role model for him. He admired Hitler's sense of superiority and belief that others were merely 'maggots' to be rid of on the planet.

He considered himself an intellectual and would pretentiously parade books around his workplace to illustrate how educated he was. He was particularly drawn to the writings of the Marquis de Sade, and other sadistic authors. The Marquis de Sade was a French nobleman whose perverse sexual preferences and erotic writings gave rise to the term sadism. Brady, like de Sade, practised sexual abuse and unnatural acts and brutality. He made a practice of violently beating up and biting repeatedly Myra Hindley, his girlfriend, and enjoyed taking photographs of her bruised and beaten body in compromising positions. She enjoyed posing for pornographic photos for him. It was her unquestioning acceptance of him that encouraged Brady to become even more extreme. He clearly understood his power over her, which led him to believe that the couple should experience the 'supreme pleasure'. The supreme pleasure would be found in the rape and murdering of others.

Brady read Harold Robins' novel 'The Carpet Baggers' to Myra. He portrayed its sickeningly detailed description of the rape of a 15-year-old, and paedophilia, as 'adventures'. He came to understand through her subservience that she would certainly comply with his wish to experience these 'adventures'. In his conceived world, only their rules mattered, and he was eager to venture into this arena of 'supreme pleasure' with his new soulmate. He had finally found a partner with whom he could perform the perfect crime.

Next, he gave her a book called 'Compulsion', about the real life abduction and killing of a Chicago schoolboy by two good-looking wealthy young men who thought they had committed the perfect crime. The novel was intended to be an argument against capital punishment, but Brady used it to work out what the killers did wrong. He explained to Myra how they made the fatal mistake of abducting the boy too close to where they lived, dumping the body in a drainage ditch where it would easily and eventually be found, and when they attempted to burn the victim's face, they didn't do it properly, so the victim was readily identifiable.

Brady was clever, sly, and meticulous. By learning from others' mistakes, he was clearly not going to make stupid and careless errors such as these. He was always confident that they would never get caught. Unfortunately, he liked to boast too much, and trusted a potential accomplice called David Smith as someone under his wing, following him with blind allegiance, like Myra. It was his arrogance and trust in his own perception that led to this fatal flaw. David Smith was not who Brady thought he was. He didn't have the killer instinct that Brady shared with Hindley.

Crime and Punishment, by Dostoyevsky, was another of Brady's favourites. It portrays a young man, Raskolnikov, who is short of money, and talks to himself, but is also handsome, proud, and intelligent. He plots a murder and has a drinking problem, similar to

Brady. (Some considered Brady an alcoholic, and he even learned to make his own alcohol as a young man). Also, like Brady, Raskolnikov commits his murder with an axe. It could be surmised that after reading this book, Brady got some ideas for his master plan of murder, and undoubtedly related to Raskolnikov and his sense of being an outsider, yet above the masses. Murder became a kind of entitlement to them.

He greatly admired Nietzsche's philosophy of the 'will to power' and the master morality; he believed that certain men, or supermen, could rise above society's moral standards, and do as they pleased. Brady embraced this concept of 'Übermensch', or superman, as the creator of new values. It becomes a solution to the problem of the death of God and nihilism. If the Übermensch acts to create new values within the moral vacuum of nihilism, there is nothing that this creative act would not justify. Alternatively, in the absence of this creation, there are no grounds upon which to criticise or justify any action, including the particular values created and the means by which they are made known. Brady felt above those around him, and by abiding by this philosophy that championed cruelty and torture, he embraced the idea that superior creatures had the right to control (and destroy if necessary) weaker ones. Due to his belief system, he felt no remorse in committing his crimes.

All these influences helped to shape the sick individual that Ian Brady would become, and undoubtedly contributed to his deviant and murderous behaviour.

Criminal Activity

Brady had a long string of criminal activity before the Moors murders, and was constantly in and out of the court system and periodically in jail. At the age of 13, Brady had his first appearance in juvenile court. He was charged with burglary and housebreaking. On the first two occasions he was arrested he was given probation, but the third time was different. He had a girlfriend at the time, Evelyn Grant, but their relationship ended when he threatened her with a flick knife after she visited a dance with another boy. He again appeared before the court, but this time with nine charges against him. It was shortly before his 17th birthday and the court put him on probation on the condition that he went to live with his mother, who had by then moved to Manchester and married an Irish fruit merchant named Pat Brady, who got him a job as a fruit porter at Smithfield Market.

Brady again resorted to thieving, and within a year of moving to Manchester, he was caught with a sack full of lead seals he had stolen and was trying to smuggle out of the market. Because he was still under 18, he was sentenced to two years in borstal for 'training'. He was initially sent to Hatfield, but after being discovered drunk on alcohol he had brewed, he was moved to the much tougher unit at Hull in Strangeways Prison.

Prison life served to harden him and he used the time of his incarceration to educate himself about crime. While incarcerated, Brady also learned illegal techniques for acquiring money, and entertained grandiose fantasies of becoming a big-time criminal, pulling off money-making bank heists.

Released on 14 November 1957, Brady returned to Manchester, where he took a labouring job, which he hated, and was dismissed from another job in a brewery. Deciding to 'better himself', Brady obtained a set of instruction manuals on bookkeeping from a local public library. His parents were struck by his studiousness; he studied alone in his room for hours on end. In early 1959, just three months after being released from borstal, Brady applied for and was offered a clerical job at Millwards Merchandising, a wholesale chemical distribution company based in Gorton. His colleagues found him to be a quiet, punctual, but short-tempered young man. He read books such as *Teach Yourself German*, and *Mein Kampf*, as well as works on Nazi atrocities. He rode a Tiger Cub motorcycle, which he used to visit the Pennines.

Experience

As a Scot exiled in an English city, Brady's compounded feelings of isolation and hostility began to manifest in other ways. Following his release from prison, he would often spend hours in his room, absorbing books about torture and sadomasochism and other methods relating to domination and servitude, as well as listening to music. Around this time, he took on a job as a butcher's assistant, and many have surmised that the experience of regularly cutting meat away from bone may have nurtured his growing interest in the physical acts of mutilation and murder. He also began drinking heavily and frequenting the cinema, and often found himself in need of extra spending money to support these new habits. Brady also gambled on horse races.

Myra Hindley

In January 1961, he met Myra Hindley, who had just been hired at Millwards as a shorthand typist. He had no particular interest in Myra, and barely noticed her for an entire year. She, however, was infatuated with him and what seemed to her to be his sophisticated ways. She was intent on snaring him, and many considered her downright obsessed. Using her wily ways, she finally caught his attention by carrying her own books to work. This drew his attention and finally, at the Christmas office party, relaxed by a few drinks, Brady asked Hindley for a date.

The relationship between Brady and Hindley soon grew into a romance, and developed while Brady was increasingly absorbed with Nazi-era atrocities and his growing sadomasochistic sexual appetite. Hindley was an eager and enthusiastic student, and under his influence, she stopped going to church and started hating children, two things that were very dear to her heart beforehand.

Shortly after they became a couple, Brady and Hindley began planning a series of bank robberies, which they never carried out. When Brady became fascinated with the idea of rape and murder for sexual gratification, Hindley actively participated in procuring child victims, as well as sexually abusing, torturing and murdering them. It was ironic that her beloved dog was named 'Puppet', as that was exactly what she came to be, a puppet to Brady.

Brady was an avid photographer and set up his own darkroom. With the aid of a time-delay camera, Brady and Hindley set about taking photographs of themselves acting out sadomasochistic fantasies. They schemed to enter into the illicit amateur pornography market, selling obscene photographs of their bizarre sexual antics with one another, but this imagined enterprise never got off the ground.

Following the murders, they would take pictures of each other standing or kneeling at the moorland burial sites of their victims. Hindley later claimed that Brady had taken the compromising pictures of her while she was unconscious, and subsequently used them to blackmail her into participating in the murders. Brady, however, has strenuously denied this suggestion and claims that Hindley was always a willing and enthusiastic participant in both the photographs and the murders. Experts and police investigators who examined the photographs claim that Hindley appeared to be a fully complicit camera subject, and seemed to relish being photographed.

The Mind of a Serial Killer

Ian Brady had many of the classic components that make up the mind of a serial killer. Edmund Kemper, a serial killer from the USA, is quoted as saying,

'It was an urge. ... a strong urge, and the longer I let it go the stronger it got, to where I was taking risks to go out and kill people — risks that normally, according to my little rules of operation, I wouldn't take because they could lead to arrest.'

This 'urge', as Kemper refers to it, is a powerful and ultimately lethal component in the mind of a serial killer. The more Brady thought about the perfect murder, the more hungry to pull it off he became. His appetite to murder became ever more urgent with time, and he had an eager and willing accomplice in gullible Hindley.

A psychopathic killer appears to lack a morality or social programming that are internal blocks to a rational or moral person. Classic characteristics attributed to serial killers are an unstable childhood, sense of abandonment, addiction to pornography, voices in their heads that encourage them to murder, prison sentences, and in severe cases such as the notorious John Wayne Gacy, he turned the blame around and claimed that the victims deserved to die. Brady seems to have shared this notion that his victims deserved to die, but for different reasons. His utter indifference to his victims seemed to override his appeal to pinpoint anyone in particular. He didn't hold a grudge against any of his innocent victims. They had bore him no offence; they were merely innocent enough to be available for an easy kill. His modus operandi seemed to be more about the accomplishment and getting away with it than anything else. Of course, the sexual abuse component was involved in each case, but it wasn't targeted towards any particular individual. He simply wanted to get away with the crime and feel above the law. This fit well into his sentiments about superiority and class. He considered himself well above the masses and scourge of society.

The most chilling fact about serial killers is that they are rational and calculating, and Brady fits that mould perfectly. As the murderer Dennis Nilsen put it, 'a mind can be evil without being abnormal'.

The FBI defines serial murder as:

- A minimum of three to four victims, with a "cooling off" period in between.

- The killer is usually a stranger to the victim – the murders appear unconnected or random.

- The murders reflect a need to sadistically dominate the victim.

- The murder is rarely "for profit"; the motive is psychological, not material.

- The victim may have "symbolic" value for the killer; method of killing may reveal this meaning.

- Killers often choose victims who are vulnerable (prostitutes, runaways, etc.)

Brady fits this definition to a tee. Additionally, statistically, the average serial killer is a white male from a lower-to-middle-class background, usually in his twenties or thirties, many of whom were physically or emotionally abused by parents. As with Brady, some were adopted or fostered, and as children, fledgling serial killers often set fires, commit petty crimes, and torture animals. Some are very intelligent and have shown great promise as successful professionals. They are also fascinated with the police and authority in general.

Getting Away with Murder

A serial killer typically has the unique ability to wear a mask. Nobody suspected Brady, or even Hindley, of behaving unusually or untoward at the time of their murdering spree. Neighbours considered them polite enough, even if they seemed to keep to themselves. Nobody ever detected any kind of deviant behaviour that would arouse suspicion. They kept well under the radar screen.

Typically, it is the mentally ill we tend to avoid, sidestepping the dishevelled, unshaven man who rants on over some private outrage. Brady certainly was aware of this inclination, and knew that he could remain undetected by appearing sophisticated, well dressed, and generally polite to the outside world. He saw it time and time again, and understood that he could blend in without notice, camouflaged in contemporary anonymity. This is the brilliant strategy that serial killers naturally use, consciously or perhaps not even cognisant of their disguise. They are the ones lurking in churches and malls, and prowling the freeways and streets. 'Dress him in a suit and he looks like ten other men', said one attorney in describing the infamous serial killer, Jeffery Dahmer. Like all evolved predators, Brady knew how to stalk his victims by gaining their trust. Serial killers don't wear their hearts on their sleeves. Instead, they hide behind a carefully constructed facade of normality.

Mask of Sanity

Because of their psychopathic nature, serial killers do not know how to feel sympathy for others, or even how to have relationships. Although Brady had a 'relationship' with Hindley, was she simply a perfect specimen that he could easily manipulate under his spell, or was she a convenient sexual partner that he could abuse however he wished, given that she would succumb to his every deviant wish and desire? Due to the fact that Hindley was a virgin when they began their relationship, and that she had witnessed plenty of physical and mental abuse from her father and mother growing up, it is no wonder that during her spellbound phase with Brady, that she was willing to try anything he suggested, no matter how abusive or scary it might have been. This was known behaviour, and she shared Brady's penchant for the daring and brutal aspects of life.

Serial killers learn how to simulate normal behavior by observing others. It is all a manipulative act, designed to entice people into their trap. Serial killers are actors with a natural ability to perform and seduce. Henry Lee Lucas described being a serial killer as 'being like a movie-star … you're just playing the part'. Although Brady didn't succumb to dressing up like someone that he wasn't, or pretending to be someone other than the man that he appeared to be, he was the master of deception when it came to luring his bait into his realm. He was manipulative to the extreme, and had a fine actress as his counterpart, Myra, his mate and his siren that convinced his victims that they were indeed in safe hands when asked to help look for a lost glove or to help moving boxes. Of course, he had the additional factor in his favour that all of his victims were innocent youths in their teens. They were trusting and compliant, and by their descriptions from friends and family, basically sweet and promising individuals striving for the greater good. Brady was utterly indifferent to their personalities, their families, or their innocence. He was on a mission to commit the perfect murder and never be caught, and nothing was going to get in his way.

The most coveted role of roaming psychopaths is a position of authority. They have an overdriving need to feel important, and strive to be a role model, one to be extolled and admired. Although Brady never really was acquainted with his victims to any large degree, he felt he easily had access to his victims, who would otherwise trust their instincts and not talk to strangers.

The Aftermath

Interestingly, when serial killers are caught, they suddenly assume a 'mask of insanity' — pretending to be a multiple personality, schizophrenic, or prone to black-outs — anything to evade responsibility. Even when they pretend to truly reveal themselves, they are still locked into playing a role. Brady's stance seemed to be one of indifference. He maintained his innocence for a while, trying to pinpoint the murder on David Smith, but then finally confessed to a couple of the murders.

'What's one less person on the face of the earth anyway?' Ted Bundy's chilling rationalisation demonstrates the how serial killers truly think. 'Bundy could never understand why people couldn't accept the fact that he killed because he wanted to kill', said one FBI investigator.

Imprisonment

After 19 years in a mainstream prison, and at one point befriending serial poisoner and fellow Nazi aficionado Graham Frederick Young, Brady was declared mentally ill in 1985, and sent to a mental hospital.

The judge at his trial determined that Brady would never reform, describing him as 'wicked beyond belief' - and effectively gave him little hope of ever being released. Successive Home Secretaries have agreed with that decision, while Lord Lane (the former Lord Chief

Justice), set a 40-year-minimum term in 1982. In 1990, Brady was informed by Home Secretary David Waddington, that both he and Hindley should never be freed.

Brady always insisted that he never wanted to be released. He frequently attempted suicide, and thought that he should be released from life, and had to be force-fed repeatedly while going on hunger strikes throughout his prison term. In September 1999, the High Court refused him the right to starve himself to death.

In early 2006, various newspapers reported that Brady was hospitalised and didn't have much longer to live. He is, however, still alive at present, and currently being held at Ashworth Hospital in Liverpool. Although it is unlikely that Brady could ever be released, and in the event that he was he would almost certainly be immediately arrested, tried and convicted for the murders of Pauline Reade and Keith Bennett, two murders which he was never charged with.

The Gates of Janus

Ian Brady's book about serial killing, 'The Gates of Janus' was published by the underground American publishing firm, Feral House, in 2001. Although it addresses the analysis of serial murder and specific serial killers, he never addresses his own offences, and it sparked outrage when announced in Britain.

Brady (and his murders) still provide headlines for the UK tabloid press, despite the many years since his incarceration. Fellow prisoner

Linda Calvey told the *The Daily Mirror* that, before her death in November 2002, Hindley confessed to the killing of a young female hitchhiker.

Brady supposedly devised a secret code to stop the police from finding out where the body of Keith Bennett is buried, and he was apparently furious that a drama documentary based on the murder was shown on ITV1 in May 2006. He bragged to various newspapers that he had previously stopped four other films from being made.

Considered by most well written, Brady's 'The Gates of Janus' provides authorities as well as laymen, with excellent criminal profiling in ways unexplored in books by forensic experts from the FBI. His publisher claims that 'on some level Ian Brady plays games with the reader.' This would be in perfect accordance to the profile of actor/serial killer.

What Makes a Serial Killer Tick?

Forensic psychiatrists and FBI agents have tried with great effort to get inside the killer's mind. Traditional explanations include childhood abuse, genetics, chemical imbalances, brain injuries, exposure to traumatic events, and perceived societal injustices. The frightening implication is that a huge population has been exposed to one or more of these traumas. Is there some sort of lethal concoction that sets serial killers apart from the rest of the population?

The Troubled child

Most people believe they have control over their impulses – no matter how angry we get, there is something that stops us from taking our aggressions out on others. Theories abound that there are probably some moral safety latches lacking in serial killers, or that they are being controlled by something unfathomable. 'I wished I could stop but I could not. I had no other thrill or happiness', said Dennis Nilsen, who wondered if he was truly evil. Sick as they undeniably are, research is demonstrating that serial killers are on the rise. Through extensive research and interviews with five notorious serial killers, author Joel Norris suggests that we are in the midst of a serial killer 'epidemic'. He also asserts that these killers have specific biological and genetic makeups that can be identified as early as five years of age.

According to Norris, there are six phases of the serial killer's cycle:

1. The Aura Phase, where the killer begins losing grip on reality;

2. The Trolling Phase, when the killer searches for a victim;

3. The Wooing Phase, where the killer lures his victim in;

4. The Capture Phase, where the victim is entrapped;

5. The Murder or Totem phase, which is the emotional high for killers; and finally,

6. The Depression Phase, which occurs after the killing.

Brady never seemed to really get what he had hoped for out of the murders, and perhaps felt emptiness and hopelessness afterwards. Serial killers often suffer from a 'post-homicidal depression. 'The killer is simply acting out a ritualistic fantasy ... but, once sacrificed, the victims identity within the murderer's own fantasy is lost. The victim no longer represents what the killer thought he or she represented. The image of a fiancee who rejected the killer, the echo of the voice of the hated mother, or the taunting of the distant father; all remain vividly in the killer's mind after the crime. Murder has not erased or changed the past because the killer hates himself even more than he did before the climax of emotion ... it is only his own past that is acted out. He has failed again. ... Instead of reversing the roles of his childhood, the killer has just reinforced them, and by torturing and killing a defenseless victim, the killer has restated his most intimate tragedies.'

Criminologist Colin Wilson, who wrote the foreword to Brady's own book, describes it thus: 'The simple truth seems to be that in most cases of folie à deux, neither partner would be capable of murder if it were not for the stimulus of the other. Some strange chemical reaction seems to occur, like a mixture of nitric acid and glycerine that makes (explosive) nitroglycerine.' This certainly seemed to be the case with Brady and Hindley. They were 'tied at the hip', and many suspect that they couldn't have acted alone, or at least not Hindley.

Brady certainly appears to fit perfectly into the serial killer profile. His own intimate tragedies unfortunately snuffed out the lives of innocent, young hopefuls.

The Troubled child

Chapter 2

Myra Hindley – The Early Years

Myra Hindley – The Early Years

Myra would grow into a striking-looking woman, but in her mid-teens the boys in her area did not consider her attractive, and she was teased with the nickname "Square Arse" because of her large-boned, and slightly masculine figure; in a year or two she would learn to dress in a way that suited her shape. She was a very ordinary teenage girl, however, much sought-after by the neighbours for babysitting because she was known to be particularly reliable, and patient with babies and toddlers.

Can we learn from a murderer's childhood what aspects of their experience contributed to their becoming violent? Are their early years a cipher that gives us real insight into the making of a killer? Or are some people simply born evil?

It is often said that hindsight is 20/20. Psychologists and other professionals point to the abuse and poverty often prevalent in the backgrounds of those who turn to the dark side. They say that killers are made, not born, and point to cold, neglectful mothers and abusive fathers.

However, the reality is that many serial killers and other villains of the worst sort have perfectly ordinary childhoods, or at least suffered no worse deprivations than millions of others who have grown up to lead blameless lives.

Still, perhaps by exploring the backgrounds of the men and women whom we fear the most, we can see at least some of the pieces of the jigsaw.

A Very Ordinary Child

In 1938, a young couple from the gritty industrial city of Manchester fell in love. They married in 1940, by which stage the Second World War was in full swing and Britain in the thick of it.

While Nellie Maybury – who was also known by her pet name, Hettie, was a Protestant, Bob Hindley had been brought up Catholic. The difference didn't seem to matter much, as neither was particularly religious. They had married in a registry office, despite the fact that this was not considered sufficient by the Catholic Church, who regarded the offspring of all such marriages, as effectively illegitimate.

When war broke out, Bob had been called up. He would serve as a paratrooper for the duration of the war. Nellie continued to work as a machinist. Bob had occasional periods of leave home from the army, and on one of these, Nellie fell pregnant.

The birth of the healthy girl baby, about two years after the wedding, took place in Crumpsall Hospital on 23 July 1942, and was apparently unexceptional. Shortly afterwards, Nellie brought her baby home to the little house in Gorton, a working-class area, where she was renting.

The baby girl was baptised into the Catholic Church. Partly because of the large numbers of Irish who had settled in the area, Manchester had a large and thriving Catholic population. The baptism, which took place on August 16, had been at Bob's insistence. Nellie had agreed on the condition that her child would be sent to a state, rather than a Catholic school, as she suspected that the Catholic teachers were more interested in imparting the catechism than in providing their charges with a good education. "Myra", the name they chose, was a common one at the time, and one that had been popular for several generations. It has been little used since the 1960s – for obvious reasons.

As the war was still ongoing, Bob fought for three more years, in North Africa, Cyprus, and Italy, serving with the Parachute Regiment and gaining a reputation as someone who was tough, hard and fearless. So that Nellie would not have to deal with the baby on her own, her mother, Ellen Maybury – who would be known as "Gran" to Myra – came to stay with her for the duration of the conflict. However, by all accounts Myra was a placid, happy baby and very easy to care for, bringing great joy to the lives of her mother and grandmother at a difficult time in their lives as a family, and in Britain as a whole.

Gran had also been married to a soldier, Peter Maybury, who had been killed in the First World War. Nellie must have been anxious that she, too, would be widowed and left to fend for herself in a society that was often very hard on a single woman. Women were still routinely paid far less than men for the same or equivalent work, and a woman on her own often found it even more difficult than everyone else to make ends meet.

While Nellie and her family were spared the worst of the war, there were regular raids on the industrial complexes in and around

Manchester, and the family sought shelter more than once in the large shelter at the end of the street, which catered to everyone living there. For baby Myra, the piercing wail of the air-raid siren must have been a very familiar sound, as it was for all the children growing up in and around Britain's major cities. While fear was a constant visitor to Gorton, and the possibility that each air raid would bring death, was known, and raids were so frequent that they acquired a strange sense of normality.

While perhaps not everybody liked him, as a soldier, Bob garnered considerable respect. He was known for being tough and violent, but also fearless and hardworking. It seemed that he had found his niche in the army, and while nobody really enjoys war, at least Bob was good at it.

When the war ended, Bob came home to his young wife, his baby girl, and a very uncertain future. He and Nellie moved to a new house, just around the corner from Gran. The location was convenient, but the house was in appalling condition, and they didn't have enough money to do very much about it. They were living at 20 Eaton Street, a working-class neighbourhood characterised by narrow streets of two-up two-down red brick houses.

Gorton was the sort of area where women, dressed in housecoats, scrubbed down the front porch, gossiped with their neighbours, and did their best to keep the household going, while the men worked hard and drank even harder. Life was tough, and most people's horizons were narrow. Few people had travelled far, holidays were almost unknown, and most families lived simply, from one pay packet to the next. The man who managed to put aside enough insurance money to pay for his own funeral was considered a success.

Little Myra had been born into a difficult family. Space was very tight in the house, and Myra didn't have her own bedroom. Instead, she slept in a narrow cot next to her parents' double bed.

Bob was a heavy drinker who came home late and often picked an argument with Nellie, who did her best to retaliate and hold her own. There were many days when Nellie took out her frustration with her husband on her child, shouting and slapping Myra.

We can only speculate as to the psychological scars the war might have left on Bob; there was little understanding of post-traumatic stress syndrome in those days. It must have been difficult for Bob to adjust to civilian life after the war; it was hard for many men. Almost overnight his circumstances had changed dramatically and in some ways for the worse. In the war, he had known every day that there was a risk that he would die, but Bob had been a hero; he had been fighting for king and country and had earned the respect of his fellow soldiers. The newspapers might never have mentioned him by name, but they frequently referenced the courage and valour of the ordinary soldiers who were putting their lives on the line to protect their country and save Europe from the scourge of Nazism.

As a civilian, instead, all Bob was qualified to do was a series of menial jobs, and he was rarely given a second glance in the street.

Back in Gorton he was just one more man with a chip on his shoulder and too little money in his pocket.

Little Myra was already three when Bob came home for good, and was nervous around her father, who must have seemed like a stranger to her. She was used to an all-female household and the kisses and hugs of her beloved Gran. Was her initial diffidence as a small child off-putting to Bob? It certainly seems to have flavoured how he treated her when she was growing up.

Working on a building site, Bob was involved in a bad accident that left him lame, and must have further embittered him. He walked with a characteristic limp, his job prospects had been hampered, and he looked older than his years. It was all a far cry from the heroism of his army exploits.

Growing up a Gorton Girl

While Bob certainly had his problems, Nellie wasn't always an easy woman herself. It wasn't all Bob's fault, but it was undeniably hard being married to someone who spent most of his pay on drink, and was quick to resort to fisticuffs. Nellie never knew when Bob was going to come home drunk, or in a foul mood, or both, and start to hit her. "Domestic violence" hadn't been invented in the Britain of the 1950s; many women went into marriage knowing that the occasional rough treatment was part and parcel of the deal they had signed up for.

Nellie always nagged Bob about how little money he had left for her to run the household. Bob felt emasculated by her words, both angry with her and with himself for not being able to provide better for the family. Inevitably, this led to a flurry of punches. When Nellie started to cry out in pain, Myra and her grandmother, who had been waiting for this moment, huddled against the living room door, and would rush in to protect her from her drunk, abusive husband. Myra would cling to her father's legs and beat them with her little fists, crying as she did so, while her Gran did her best to calm him down and get Nellie away from him.

While Myra was often beaten by her father, too, her mother was also frequently violent, turning on her child at the slightest provocation. While this was all undoubtedly traumatic for a little girl, it should be noted that domestic violence was not uncommon in the working-class area the Hindley family lived in. Many young wives and mothers simply accepted a degree of violence as a normal and natural part of family life. In an article published in The Guardian on 18 December 1995, Myra Hindley herself was quoted as saying:

Friday and Saturday nights were known as "wife beating" nights: the men worked hard all week and many spent the weekends drinking. Pub closing times were dreaded because we all knew what would happen. Women ran out into the street, trying to escape from being beaten. All of the kids used to jump out of bed and run outside to try to stop our fathers hurting our mothers, and we were often turned on too.

While Myra was very close to her Gran, she did not bond with the grandparents on her father's side of the family. Bob's parents were not at all like the gentle Ellen Maybury, and Myra's difficult relationship with them contributed to her father's growing resentment of her. The fact that she bore him a close physical resemblance didn't seem to help at all.

In 1946, Myra's younger sister Maureen was born. Maureen was a pretty little baby who looked quite different than Myra, who was already tall for her age. For all her own problems, Nellie realised that there was now a serious risk that Myra would come to real harm. Without the baby to distract her, she had always been able to stop Bob from being unduly harsh with his daughter. But now that she had a younger child to care for, could she vouch for Myra's safety? She arranged for her to go and live with her Gran, whose home was on nearby Beasley Street. Nobody thought that this would have had a deleterious impact on the little girl. After all, Ellen spent most of her time caring for Myra anyway, and everybody knew how close they were.

While Myra loved her grandmother, she was desperately upset about being sent away from home; these feelings of rejection would never leave her. She continued to eat her meals in the family home with her parents, where her father often told her – and demonstrated – how she should stand up for herself when she was bullied. Myra quickly learned that the only way in which she could earn her father's respect was by becoming physically tough, just as he was. Perhaps Bob was trying to turn Myra into the son he didn't have.

Myra often got into fights, with boys as well as girls, and was well able to stand up for herself. This was partly because she was big for her age, but more because she didn't flinch when she was hurt, and had no qualms about inflicting pain on others. She quickly earned a reputation as a child who would fight to the end, and wasn't afraid of anyone.

Myra attended Peacock Street Primary School when she was five, in 1947. She was quick with her lessons and generally liked by the teachers. With a little more encouragement at home, Myra could have done very well. However, her grandmother Ellen often let her stay away from school, which had inevitable consequences for her academic performance.

Ellen, who was not highly educated herself, simply didn't understand how a good education could make all the difference in a child's life, and especially in the life of a little girl growing up in a community that was dominated by men and their needs and desires. Ellen was from a generation that believed that each person was born into a particular social class, and stayed there.

In letting Myra out of school as often as she did, Ellen was showing, in her mistaken way, how much she loved and indulged her granddaughter. She was also giving her a lesson about responsibility; namely, that it was there to be shirked whenever possible.

Although the war was over, Britain was continuing an austerity drive. Food was still rationed and things were tight for most families.

drive. Food was still rationed and things were tight for most families. In Gorton, where things had always been tight anyway, war or no war, there was very little extra money to go around.

Beginning to Grow Up

When Myra was eight, one of the neighbouring children scratched her badly, leaving painful, bleeding scrapes on her face. She ran to her parents for comfort, but her father told her that if she would not stand up for herself, he would beat her. Still crying, Myra found the boy who had hurt her and knocked him over, standing above him in triumph while a gaggle of local children watched, gawping with their little mouths open. She would remember this as a seminal moment in her early life. Bob was very proud of Myra for standing up for herself and showered her with praise. Finally Myra had learned what she needed to do in order to earn her father's respect. Was this a turning point for her?

While Bob didn't protest against Nellie's insistence that Myra attend a state, rather than a Catholic school, his family ensured that Myra and her sister were familiar with the Catholic Church and its rites; Myra often attended Mass together with her Aunt Kate, Bob's sister. Myra enjoyed the dark, atmospheric interior of the local church and the rich, evocative scent of the incense burned during the ceremony. In those pre-Vatican Two days, the Catholic Mass was still read in Latin, which brought a touch of the exotic to a very ordinary Gorton lass's weekly life.

As she started to grow up and approach adolescence, Myra rebelled against her abusive parents, refusing to do as she was told, and showing that she was never going to be easy to manage. This often caused the violence from her father to escalate; he didn't seem to realise that his own unruly behaviour was simply being echoed in his daughter's. By this stage, however, Myra was so used to being slapped around the head and beaten, that it didn't have much impact on her – or so it seemed. Young Myra's relationship with her father was complex; on the one hand, she was often angry with and scared of him. On the other, she bore a strong physical resemblance to him – one that was often remarked upon. She yearned for his approval, but scorned and looked down on his lack of control at the same time.

Despite her tendency to be rough, Myra was a bright child who loved to read and devoured children's classics such as anything by Beatrix Potter and Enid Blyton, as well as Arthur Ransome's *Swallows and Amazons*, despite the fact that the lives of the "posh" children in the stories could not have been more unlike her own experience. She particularly loved *The Secret Garden* by Frances Hodgson Burnett, which tells the story of a little girl who makes an abandoned garden bloom on the wild and windy moors.

By the end of primary school, Myra had entered puberty and experienced a dramatic growth spurt; she was already far taller than any of her friends, and received the moniker "Beanstalk" as a result. Even at this early age, it was time for her to start thinking about her future. Because of her gift for creative writing and the ease with which she carried out her studies, she was put forward for the

11-plus exam. If she had passed it, this would have enabled her to go to grammar school, and perhaps in time move beyond the grimness of her home life. For many bright young people from working-class backgrounds, the 11-plus was a passport to university or another form of higher education, and a middle-class life. With all that responsibility on her young shoulders, Myra panicked and failed. Her grandmother's tendency to keep her home instead of making sure that she went to school certainly did not help.

Rather than going to grammar school, Myra was enrolled in a local Secondary Modern, Ryder Brow. This must have been galling for a child who knew that she was clever, even if a little undisciplined. Although she often missed days at school, she was in the top academic stream, and was still notably good at the creative writing at which she had excelled in primary school. She was good at sports, too; tall and strong enough to play alongside the boys, and fiercely competitive – so much so that she could become quite angry if one of her teammates let the side down. She had started smoking and was quite open about the boys she fancied, although her social brashness belied the fact that, in some ways, she was still very naïve and inexperienced.

Death Enters Myra's Life

When Myra was fifteen years old, real tragedy came into her life. It had started as an ordinary day, and ended when her friend Michael Higgins had gone swimming in a local waterhole, Mellands Fields

Reservoir, and drowned. The reservoir was known to be dangerous and all the children in the area had been warned more times than they could count to stay away from it. A number of locals had committed suicide by throwing themselves into its murky depths, and only the most daring of the local teenagers would swim there. The water was thick with green weed and algae that was reputed to become entangled around ankles and wrists and pull unwary swimmers into a watery grave.

Myra and Michael had swum together at the reservoir often; she was such a strong swimmer that she had no fear for either herself or her friend. But on this particular day, when Michael had suggested that they visit the reservoir, Myra had decided to go into town. Michael had gone swimming with two other boys instead, neither of whom was able to save him when he started getting into difficulties. Apparently they had assumed that he was joking around when he started thrashing in the water. By the time they realised that he had really got into difficulties, it was too late. Michael's slender body had already sunk to the bottom of the water, from which it would be retrieved later, by a diver.

Michael, who lived nearby, had been one of Myra's very closest friends. Two years younger than her, he had been a rather delicate and "soft" child who had often had good reason to be grateful to the older, very protective Myra, who had cosseted and cared for him. In many ways she behaved more like a mother or an aunt, than a friend and a peer. Despite the fact that Michael went to the local Catholic school and Myra was at the state-run Secondary Modern,

Myra Hindley – the Early Years

they spent all their free time talking and having fun, with Myra very much the leader in the relationship. Seeing the two young people together, their families often commented on how Myra treated Michael as though he were the younger brother she had never had. She was particularly pleased about the fact that they had the same initials, which seemed to her to have some special, mystical significance.

Now that Michael was gone, Myra blamed herself for not having been there – Michael had invited Myra to go swimming with him and went out with another friend instead. It was as if she had inadvertently set a curse on him by so casually rejecting his invitation. Myra, an athletic girl and a strong swimmer, was sure that she would have been able to save Michael – and she was probably right. After all, they had gone swimming there together on many occasions, and he had never come to any harm.

While Myra was distraught by Michael's death, her friends noticed that she was oddly fascinated to see Michael's body laid out for his funeral with his pale, cold hands twined around a set of rosary beads, according to Roman Catholic tradition. They realised how upset the young girl was, and were concerned that her loss would have a terrible impact on her. Michael's mother kindly removed the beads from her son's fingers and gave them to her as a gift to remember her friend by.

Dressed in mourning, Myra went from door to door in her locality, gathering money for a splendid funeral wreath to honour her best friend. Everyone noted how pale and pinched she looked and, although money was tight in most local homes, many of them chipped in to ensure that Michael's young life would be appropriately commemorated.

Myra shed many tears at Michael's wake and in the course of the days and weeks that followed. This surprised many of the people who knew her, as she had a reputation for being a tough girl who didn't let things get her down. Few people had ever seen her cry before. When the funeral Mass was held at the local Catholic Church, St Francis's, Myra was too distraught to go, and at the burial afterwards she stood with her back to the small crowd that had gathered to pray, as Michael's coffin was lowered into the ground. For weeks after the burial, she went every day to visit the grave, bringing Michael gifts of flowers that she had picked from the hedgerows and stolen from local gardens.

After Michael's death, Myra sought solace in the Catholic faith. Although she had been baptised into the Church as a tiny baby, she had never been an active participant. Now she took instruction in the catechism. For a long period after Michael's death, Myra dressed in black in his memory, and appeared to be completely caught up in her grief. Her family and friends became concerned about her, worrying that she was putting her life on hold and, possibly, enjoying her grief a little too much. It was normal to be upset about Michael's drowning, of course, but Myra seemed to be completely obsessed, and to want people to feel sorry for her.

A Young Lady

Following Michael's death, Myra also stopped paying much attention to her schoolwork. Despite a lack of commitment, her natural intelligence had meant that until now she had found school quite easy. Now that her attention was entirely elsewhere, her marks started to suffer. When she reached the age of fifteen, at which stage she could legally leave school, she agreed with her teachers' assessment that there was no point in her staying on to do O-levels. Despite her initial promise, it seemed that young Myra was destined to stay in the same working-class niche as her parents, and their parents before them.

Myra would grow into a striking-looking woman, but in her mid-teens the boys in her area did not consider her attractive, and she was teased with the nickname "Square Arse" because of her large-boned, and slightly masculine figure; in a year or two she would learn to dress in a way that suited her shape. She was a very ordinary teenage girl, however, much sought-after by the neighbours for babysitting because she was known to be particularly reliable, and patient with babies and toddlers.

Myra left school at a time when there was plenty of work. Manchester was then a thriving industrial area with jobs for all the young people leaving school. Myra was quickly employed as a junior clerk in an engineering company in Openshaw, Lawrence Scott and Electromotors. The economic situation had improved across Britain; for young people like Myra, the war was already a distant memory. Gone were the ration books and the constant reiteration of the necessity of "making do".

While working-class youngsters like Myra didn't have a lot of money, for the first time there was enough money left over after paying for all the basics to spend some on a pretty dress, make-up, the latest record, or a night out listening to music, smoking, and drinking. A musical revolution had started, and youngsters across Britain were expressing themselves through their love of the exciting new trends. Myra smoked Park Drives, the cigarette brand that had become synonymous with Britain's working classes. The rise in living standards penetrated even to the darkest streets of Manchester's slum areas, and the lives of people who had always scraped by started to improve. Like every other girl in the English-speaking world, Myra was madly in love with Elvis Presley, who was still slender and beautiful, and whose antics on the stage had earned him the nickname "Elvis the Pelvis". Older people didn't approve of the singers overtly sexual antics, but youngsters like Myra lapped it all up. "Free love" was just around the corner, and Elvis seemed to epitomise the new spirit of adventure. Myra liked to jive; it was all the rage at the time and it was a dance she could enjoy without feeling self-conscious about being much taller than her male partner.

Still only fifteen, Myra longed to be taken seriously by the slightly older boys she found attractive. When one of her colleagues at work suggested that she bleach her hair, she jumped at the opportunity. Her hair was naturally mid-brown and not very glamorous. With her hair bleached almost white, and coiffed in the latest beehive style, Myra looked much older than her years and very in keeping with the fashion of the day. Her mother told her that she looked cheap, but

Myra didn't care; she'd found her look and she was determined to stick with it.

As well as music, Myra liked dances and going to the cinema, and, although she was conservative in her sexual behaviour and would remain a virgin until she met Ian Brady, was interested in boys. Myra had seen what happened to girls who got pregnant young, and the last thing she wanted was to find herself stuck in a loveless marriage with a snotty brat to take care of, before she had even learned to start living.

Despite Myra's love of modern music and socialising, Myra was still very attracted to the Catholic Church. She remembered how important the faith had been to Michael's family, and the comfort she had found in it when she was mourning. She received First Holy Communion in November 1958, when she was sixteen years old. It comforted her to think that she was practising the religion that was so dear to the hearts of Michael and his family. Shortly afterwards, she became godmother to Michael's little nephew, Anthony John.

When she was seventeen, Myra was made redundant and found work as a typist for a furniture shop in Gorton. Bob had had a stroke by now, and his health was poor – however, his temper was not improved by this turn of events, and he continued to be violent and abusive to Nellie. By now, Myra had grown into her looks and was quite pretty. She attracted the attention of a local boy, to whom she became engaged.

Ronnie Sinclair, Myra's fiancé, was an ordinary working-class lad who was employed blending tea at the local co-op. He was a nice boy, just a year older than her, but when Myra looked at the humdrum lives of the young working-class couples in her area, and considered the fact that Ronnie didn't seem to have any particularly stellar prospects, she realised that she wanted more, and broke off the engagement.

Without Ronnie, Myra had considered leaving her home area, perhaps by finding work as an au pair in America, or by going into the Forces. Maybe she could build a better life. She started to study judo and was good at it, although nobody wanted to be her partner because she was so strong and always reluctant to release her grip.

Nellie was relieved by Myra's decision not to marry Ronnie. She had endured a long, difficult and largely loveless marriage herself, and didn't want the same for Myra. The girl was still young; there was plenty of time to find a nice lad and settle down.

However, the reality is that many serial killers and other villains of the worst sort have perfectly ordinary childhoods, or at least suffered no worse deprivations than millions of others who have grown up to lead blameless lives. Still, perhaps by exploring the backgrounds of the men and women whom we fear the most, we can see at least some of the pieces of the jigsaw.

Chapter 3

Millwards Merchandising

Millwards Merchandising

They both had so much to drink, that the rest of the night passed in a haze, with many of the details completely lost. When Ian dropped Myra home, they kissed for the first time, rather awkwardly. Myra could not have been happier as she staggered drunkenly up the stairs towards her room. At last, her prince had come along.

At work the next day, Myra was initially disappointed that Ian didn't behave any differently towards her than before, but he was just biding his time; in a quiet moment he drew her aside and asked her if she would like to go to the cinema with him the following weekend. Of course, Myra said 'yes'. That evening, she made a triumphant entry in her diary. She and Ian were an item. Her dream was finally coming true, and life as she knew it was about to take a very different turn.

By the age of eighteen, Myra had accumulated quite a lot of work experience; she had been working for three years. As at school, she wasn't always the most eager, but her natural intelligence ensured that her employers were usually happy with her performance, even if she tended to be surly and rather inclined to moan when things didn't go her way. Myra picked things up quickly, and had become a competent typist with quite good prospects in the increasingly upbeat economy of Manchester. While the area had been badly damaged during the war, and still bore some of the scars of that awful time, hope and prosperity had returned to Britain, and with them the chance that a bright working-class girl like Myra might gain the opportunity to develop a proper career and move up in the world. This was a time of upward social mobility, when young men and women with talent and potential started to step out of the slums they had grown up in, and move towards the leafy suburbs that had been unattainable to their parents.

An Office Girl

On 21 December 1960, Myra attended an interview at Millwards Merchandising, a long-established chemical supply business with close links to the cotton industry, cotton having been a big industry in the area since the days of the transatlantic slave trade. The company was run from a large old house on Levenshulme Road, rather dilapidated, and filled with chemicals and filing cabinets. The staff members were used to the chemical odours, but anyone coming into the building for the first time wrinkled their nose in distaste.

Despite having come down in the world, it was still easy to see the building for the gracious family home it had once been – it had generous proportions, and a rose garden ran wild outside, hinting at long summer days, and sandwiches, and tennis on the lawn. It had once been the sort of home in which the 'posh' children in the storybooks Myra had loved as a child would have lived. The new job as a typist at Millwards Merchandising was a step up in the world.

At her interview, Myra did a typing test, which she passed with no problem, and was interviewed by the company head, a friendly middle-aged man called Tom Craig. Myra showed herself to be an articulate young woman, apparently mature beyond her years, and got the job. She would be working from nine to five Monday to Friday, as well as Saturday mornings, and would be quite well paid at nearly nine pounds a week. As Myra was still living with her Gran, much of that money would be disposable income. She was doing alright for herself.

Love at First Sight

Tom was a kind boss, eager to be on good terms with all the employees, no matter how junior. He made a real effort to make Myra feel at home, despite the fact that she was rather socially awkward. Myra was shown around the office and introduced to the rest of the staff. She was immediately taken by one of the clerks, Ian Brady, who wore a stylish quiff and a devil-may-care attitude. Everyone smoked in the office in those days; when she met him, Ian had a cigarette dangling from the corner of his mouth, just like the bad boys she saw in the Hollywood films – just like James Dean! Apparently he glanced up at her and nodded to say hello, without paying her any more attention. And just like that, she was hooked, and her life had changed forever.

Years later, Myra told a journalist for The Guardian that falling for Ian had been just like her passion for movie stars and singers like Elvis Presley. 'I'd always been a dreamer', she said, 'falling in love with film stars. I was crazy about James Dean and Elvis, and had heard the phrase 'falling head over heels in love' - but never thought it would happen to me. But as soon as Ian Brady looked at me and smiled shyly, that's exactly what happened'.

A Naughty Boy

Although Ian had a criminal record and came from a family background that was even more 'difficult' than Myra's, he was very ambitious and had trained as a bookkeeper specifically to avoid having to go into manual labour, which he felt was beneath him. Although he had not achieved very much in his short life, Ian had no doubt that he was destined for greatness. In Strangeways Prison, where he was sent when he was just seventeen for having carried out a variety of petty crimes, Ian had learned tricks from other criminals, and started to fantasise about becoming a successful bank robber. But he was also pragmatic. As well as fantasising about a glorious future, he spent his time more usefully, acquiring skills as a bookkeeper. After a job carrying out menial work at a brewery, he had been hired by Millwards Merchandising as a stock clerk. This was still a rather lowly position, but at least it was a step in the right direction. He had been in the position for two years by the time Myra came on the scene.

Ian had just enough money to indulge his fascination for new technology; he had purchased recording equipment and had made vinyl copies of Hitler's speeches to listen to at home – and he had also created a darkroom so that he could develop his own photographs, starting out with a Box Brownie, a standard low-cost model that was very popular at the time, before graduating to more expensive equipment. He was fascinated with image and appearance, and this fed very much into his love of photography.

Myra's Growing Fascination

Myra found it difficult to concentrate on her work the first day in the office. Ian was in the room, and she couldn't stop herself from glancing up from her typewriter to look at him. Although he wasn't on a huge salary, he was carefully dressed in a waistcoat and tie, and had clearly gone to some effort with his appearance, unlike many of the young men in Gorton, who lolled around in their mechanics' or labourers' clothes even when they had finished working, and didn't give two hoots about the oil under their fingernails. Ian looked like a gentleman with his pressed clothes, groomed hair and carefully manicured fingernails. The fingernails impressed Myra the most. In later years she often recalled that he had been the first man she ever met with really clean nails. When he spoke, it was with a Glaswegian accent that had a touch of the exotic, especially in contrast to the flat local accent. He was formal in his manner, referring to her as 'Miss Hindley', almost as though he was much older.

But later on that same day, Myra found out that Ian wasn't always as gentlemanly as he appeared at first. All the men in the office seemed to be obsessed with horse-racing, and at lunchtime, Ian popped down to the bookies to place his bets; he had had an interest in gambling since boyhood and had a special nickname that he used to bet under – 'Gorgonzola', later abbreviated to 'Gorgon'. When he rang to get the results shortly afterwards, he found out that his horse hadn't won and threw the phone to the ground, screaming obscenities about the money he had lost and the time he had wasted in the process.

Nobody batted an eyelid, suggesting that they were used to antics of this sort from their colleague. None of this behaviour seemed strange to Myra; after all, her father and most of the men she knew had short tempers and lashed out when things didn't go their way. For all she knew, this was how all men behaved. Ian's behaviour certainly didn't do anything to dampen the flames of her crush on him.

But even if Ian's outbursts seemed par for the course, he wasn't exactly like all the other men. He loved to read, and was proud of having pored over very challenging literature. Bob, Myra's father, never read anything. Raising his voice slightly, the better to be heard by everyone within earshot, he told the staff in the office about the books he had been reading; books by authors such as the Russian Dostoevsky, the Marquis de Sade, and the German philosopher Nietzsche. Ian was also quick to tell everyone all about how he was learning German, so that he would be able to read Nietzsche in the original text. He had bought himself books to help him to acquire the language.

If Ian's intention was to impress, it worked with at least one of the people in the room; Myra knew that he was sending them the message that he was not just a lowly office clerk, but a man of the world, with a keen interest in intellectual pursuits. She heard the message loud and clear, and was inclined to agree with Ian's assessment. Ian clearly knew that he was worth better things than what Gorton, Manchester and Millwards Merchandising had to offer. Until now, Myra had never met a man who read anything other than the sports pages, or maybe a story about a hard-boiled detective, or cowboys and Indians. When he wasn't placing bets at the bookies, Ian spent his lunch break poring over *Teach Yourself German* or Hitler's *Mein Kampf*, while he ate his egg and cheese sandwich, apparently lost in his intellectual pursuits. She remembered how much she had loved to read when she was a little girl. Maybe she had finally found a man who would understand her! Ian seemed so refined and mannerly, and to know so much. Would he be able to teach her?

While Ian performed his work satisfactorily, later on the affable Tom Craig remembered having regretted hiring him. Craig always wanted the office to have a friendly atmosphere, and Ian was rather standoffish.

A Campaign to Win Ian's Heart

Myra was utterly infatuated with Ian, although he didn't give any indication of returning her interest. She found out where he lived and took to walking on his street in the hope of 'accidentally' meeting up – often taking a borrowed baby with her as a 'decoy' – but that didn't happen. For a year, she made frenzied entries in her girlish diary, all about how much she loved Ian. She lamented the fact that he seemed to be immune to her charms, and speculated about how she could get him to notice her. Years later, Myra remembered how hard she had worked to get Ian to notice her, and wrote:

That first year of working in the same office as Ian was mental torture. Sometimes he would speak to me normally, other times he ignored me completely.

I was far too proud to let him see the way I felt about him, and never showed how hurt I was when he'd been nasty to me. I wrote everything down in a diary, which I kept locked in one of my desk drawers. Sometimes I would write that I hated him because he was cold and cruel; other times I would beg God to let him love me the same way as I loved him.

Eventually, Myra decided that she would show Ian that she could be intellectual, too. Maybe in this way she would stand out from the crowd, and reveal herself to be the companion she was sure Ian needed. Like most young women her age, Myra usually read romantic pap, and magazines full of stories about meeting Mr Right, and breathless brides in frothy wedding dresses. Myra knew that Ian's opinion of such lowbrow reading matter wasn't fit to be printed. He made no secret of the fact that he thought that most people were unintelligent and beneath his attention.

Myra went to the local library and borrowed a copy of *The Collected Works of Wordsworth*. The following day, she put her plan into action.

When lunchtime came around, Myra ostentatiously withdrew her book and started to read it near where Ian was playing chess with one of the other office staff. Her plan worked; he was surprised to see her reading something so challenging, and asked her if the book was any good. When she said it was, he said he might get a copy for himself. Myra was over the moon with joy. A few days later, when Myra borrowed the poetry of William Blake and used it for her lunchtime reading, it turned out that Ian was a great fan. For Myra, this was an enormous breakthrough.

From then on, Myra made a point of bringing challenging books, often poetry, into the office and, little by little, she and Ian started to become close. They talked about books and music. Ian told her that he had his own tape recorder, which he had bought on a hire-purchase scheme, and that he liked to record things from the television. He offered to lend some of his music to her. When he asked Myra what sort of music she liked to listen to, she wasn't sure what to say, and what would impress him the most, so she told him that she enjoyed a bit of everything. Although Myra really only ever listened to the pop songs of the day, this was a good answer, because Ian responded that he liked to listen to 'clever' music – classical and the like – and that he could lend her some if she wanted. Joyfully, Myra responded that she loved classical music, it was her favourite, and she would positively adore listening to whatever Ian recommended. She rushed out and arranged to get her own tape recorder through the hire-purchase scheme so that she could enjoy whatever Ian saw fit to lend her.

Myra was in heaven. She thought that Ian was the most sophisticated man in the world. With his brains and learning, surely he would go far. Ronnie, Myra's fiancé, was ringing her all the time, begging her to get back together with him. He was so insistent that eventually Tom, the owner, told him that he would hear from the police if he didn't stop ringing the office, harassing Myra and annoying everyone. Now Myra compared the hapless Ronnie to Ian, and he came up short. Ronnie represented everything small and unambitious about life in Gorton. Ian seemed to be a portal

to another world; a world full of sophistication, elegance
and opportunity.

The Campaign Bears Fruit

The office was a friendly place. Although Myra did most of her work
isolated in a small room of her own, there was a lot of camaraderie
among the staff. They regularly went out for drinks after work, and
the men's collective love of the bookies was a running joke. Ian and
Myra finally got together at the office Christmas party. Everybody
had been drinking heavily, and Myra was on the dance floor when
Ian appeared and asked her to dance with him. Finally, her dream of
attracting his attention seemed to be coming true. As their co-workers
watched, they danced tipsily around the room, with Ian landing on
Myra's toes more often than not; he was a terrible dancer, but Myra
didn't care. Stepping around the room with Ian, she was in seventh
heaven. When the party ended, Tom asked everyone if they wanted
a lift home, and Ian announced that he would walk Myra home.
She was ecstatic, and rushed straight to a public phone to let her
girlfriends know that she wouldn't be seeing them later, as had been
the plan, because she was going out with Ian. There were a lot of
excited squeals; all her friends knew that she had been mooning over
Ian for months.

Myra and Ian continued the party on their own afterwards, drinking
even more at one of the local pubs. Whereas all the men Myra had
ever known chugged back pints of beer, Ian ordered red wine,

just like a European gentleman. Ian was full of chat, laughing and sharing jokes. He was good at doing impressions, and had Myra in stitches when he pretended to be the characters on *The Goon Show*, which was very popular at the time. *The Goon Show* was a radio comedy broadcast that had been on the air between 1951 and 1960, featuring Spike Milligan, Peter Sellers and Harry Secombe. It was based around surreal humour that made fun of aspects of life in Britain at the time, and featured innovative sound effects. *The Goon Show* had a huge listenership and Ian was a big fan. It is considered by many as a forerunner of the hugely popular series of the 1970s. Myra was one of the very few people in Britain at the time not to be extremely familiar with *The Goon Show*'s many famous characters and catchphrases, but she laughed at Ian's impersonations anyway, and didn't stop to wonder why. She was just happy to be out with him at last.

They both had so much to drink, that the rest of the night passed in a haze, with many of the details completely lost. When Ian dropped Myra home, they kissed for the first time, rather awkwardly. Myra could not have been happier as she staggered drunkenly up the stairs towards her room. At last, her prince had come along.

At work the next day, Myra was initially disappointed that Ian didn't behave any differently towards her than before, but he was just biding his time. In a quiet moment he drew her aside and asked her if she would like to go to the cinema with him the following weekend. Of course, Myra said 'yes'. That evening, she made a triumphant entry in her diary. She and Ian were an item. Her dream was finally

Moors Murderer Myra Hindley on the beach at Blackpool, Lancashire, with the Central Pier in the background, circa 1960.

i

Myra Hindley and Ian Brady posing for a self-portrait on the moor where they buried their child victims, 1960s.

A photograph of Myra Hindley, taken by Ian Brady, near the site where the couple buried Keith Bennett, 1960s.

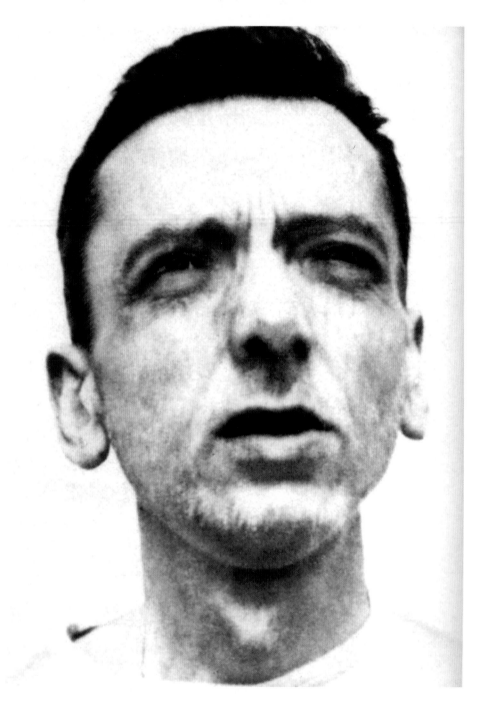

Photograph of Ian Brady, looking gaunt, 1960s.

A shot of Myra Hindley, taken by Ian Brady, near the site where the couple buried Keith Bennett, 1960s.

Myra Hindley in Cookham Wood Prison, 1960s.

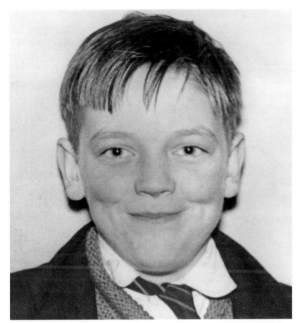

12-year-old murder victim John Kilbride, who was killed by
Moors Murderer Ian Brady, 23rd November 1963.

A photograph of Ian Brady, 1960s.

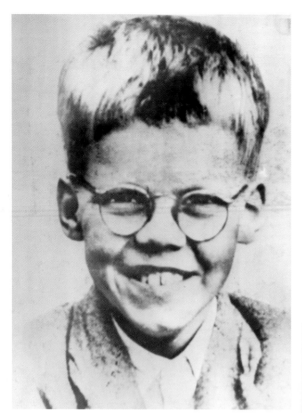

12-year-old murder victim Keith Bennett, who was killed by Moors Murderer Ian Brady, 16th June 1964. His body has not yet been found.

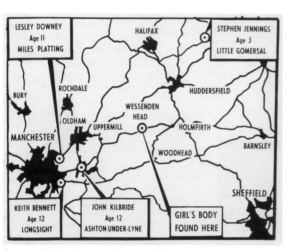

A map of Manchester and parts of Yorkshire showing where missing children, believed to be victims of the Moors Murderers, Ian Brady and Myra Hindley, lived, October 1965.

A photograph of Myra Hindley (left), circa 1965, before being convicted of two counts of murder in conjunction with her partner, Ian Brady, 1966.

coming true, and life as she knew it was about to take a very different turn.

Years later, Myra told a journalist for The Guardian that falling for Ian had been just like her passion for movie stars and singers like Elvis Presley. 'I'd always been a dreamer', she said, 'falling in love with film stars. I was crazy about James Dean and Elvis, and had heard the phrase 'falling head over heels in love' - but never thought it would happen to me. But as soon as Ian Brady looked at me and smiled shyly, that's exactly what happened'.

Chapter 4

The Fatal Attraction

The blurb on the back of 'Compulsion', a book based on the real-life story about murderers Nathan Leopold and Richard, read, 'You know why we did it? Because we damn well felt like doing it!'

This was a book that could have been written for Ian. He pored over it and was astounded by how stupidly the kidnapping and murder had been carried out. They had done everything wrong. As Ian saw it, their biggest mistake had been their appalling lack of planning.

Ian told Myra that if they were to commit the perfect murder, they would never make so many stupid mistakes. They would put in time to plan properly.

It had become clear that Ian was now ready to move away from fantasy and take a giant step towards really carrying out the awful deeds that he often talked about.

On their first real date, Myra and Ian went to see the film *King of Kings*, about the life of Jesus Christ, narrated by Orson Wells. Myra sniffled into her hankie the whole way through the dramatic retelling of one of history's most famous lives, but afterwards, walking home, Ian expounded on the fact that he hated religion, and thought that only really stupid people were taken in by it. He hated Catholicism in particular, telling Myra that Catholicism and all its trappings were for the weak-minded. He used the term 'opium of the masses'. This was shocking stuff for the girl who had chosen to take personal instruction in the catechism before making a firm commitment to the faith just a few years before.

When Myra protested weakly, and tried to stand up for the faith that had brought her so much comfort in difficult times, Ian asked her why, if God was all-powerful, he had allowed her beloved childhood friend to die. She had nothing to say to that. This was a painfully difficult question that Myra had often asked herself. In the wake of Michael's death, she had turned to the Church for comfort, and it had helped – but it hadn't brought Michael back, had it? He was still dead. Thinking about it carefully, Myra had to concede that maybe Ian had a point. Perhaps religion really was a mug's game after all.

Losing her Virginity

That night, Myra and Ian made love for the first time, downstairs on the sofa while Gran slept upstairs. Ian was an enthusiastic, but brutal lover, who treated Myra roughly, biting her more often than he kissed her. Myra had been a virgin until this moment, and Ian was not very sexually experienced either. Neither of them seemed to have found anything unusual in this approach to sex. For her, the rough treatment was an extension of how she had always been treated by her father, for whom violence was interspersed with occasional outbursts of affection. She had often almost welcomed her father's violence towards her, because at least it meant that she was not being ignored. It is hard to overlook the parallels with her experience with Ian. Myra's first experience of sex left her bruised and battered, but exultant, because it had been with the first man whom she had truly loved, and it was a deeply intimate act that had brought them closer together than ever before. Ian had shown her that they really, truly belonged together.

Being Remade in Ian's Image

Myra and Ian also went to see the film *The Nuremburg Trials*, and afterwards he advised her to start reading Hitler's work, telling her that a lot of what he had to say made perfect sense. Hitler had had no time for the inferior people of the world, and had understood that in order for real progress to be made, intelligent people needed to make some difficult, but very necessary, decisions. Myra was happy to oblige. After years of underperforming at school and at work, it must have felt good to start using her brain again.

As their relationship progressed, Myra fell increasingly under Ian's spell. She was prepared to do anything he wanted, including posing for pornographic images that he developed at home – this at a time when cultural mores about sexuality and nudity were very different to those of today. This also gave Ian power over her, or so she felt, because with photographs and negatives of Myra behaving so shamefully, he could always decide to show her friends and family, if she annoyed him in any way.

Sharing Secrets

As they grew ever closer, Ian must have told Myra all about his troubled family background. He had been born in a rough part of Glasgow, the Gorbals, on the January 1938, to a young woman, Margaret Stewart, who worked as a waitress in a tea room. Margaret never did tell Ian who his father was, and it is not unreasonable to assume that she did not know herself. Unable to cope with Ian on his own, she put him into foster care. He was a difficult child, who often returned his foster mother's care and affection with violence and irrational rages, although he had a lot of genuine affection for the family that had taken him in, and would remain in contact with them after growing up. Margaret visited him periodically, but little Ian must have felt desperately rejected – and he also had to live with the stigma associated with illegitimacy. Still, he always protested that he had had a happy childhood. His foster parents had been kind, and his mother had visited him regularly; she hadn't abandoned him, although she could have, and she often brought him gifts of clothes and toys.

Ian had been a bright and attractive child, and, like Myra, had had a vivid imagination and a particular talent for creative writing. Although he could be difficult, he had done well in school. Unlike Myra, he passed an exam that gained him entrance to a prestigious academic secondary school, Shawlands Academy. There, he had developed a love of modern history, and a fascination with the Second World War, and especially the Nazis, that would remain with him always.

Despite his academic promise, by the time he reached his teens, Ian was a tearaway, involved in petty crime and obsessed with horror films; his friends referred to him as 'Dracula' as a result. Whenever Ian had a little pocket money, he spent it on going to the cinema to see a scary film, and often watched the same one over and over again. Nothing was too scary or gruesome for him. In fact, he was often annoyed that the stories he could invent in his head were far 'better' than the ones he saw on the screen.

When he came up before the court on a number of charges, Ian was given probation for two years and sent to Manchester, where Margaret was now living with her new husband, the Irishman Patrick Brady. Ian liked Patrick, and took his surname in an effort to feel like a 'real' member of the family. Perhaps he had hoped that he would now experience some stability in his life, but of course he didn't – he soon drifted back into the petty crime and general delinquency that had been part of who he was for as long as he could remember. But on his last stint in prison, he'd realised that these small-time crimes weren't going to get him anywhere. He studied for, and received an elementary qualification, in bookkeeping.

Ian told Myra all about his criminal record, but it didn't put her off – he was a reformed character, wasn't he – and anyway, plenty of the men in Gorton had been in trouble with the law. Being involved in petty crime, and even serving time now and again, was a concept familiar to anyone from Gorton. Besides, Ian was so clever and well-read, that she could see for herself how he was on the way up in the world. He couldn't have been more different to Ronnie, whom Myra saw now as not being worth anything. She had dismissed poor Ronnie and the normal, ordinary life he offered – marriage, family, and a quiet home life – as though he was nothing more than a piece of litter stuck to her shoe.

Myra's family life hadn't been easy, but at least she had had her parents and her Gran and knew that they loved her, even if her mum and dad had sometimes shown it in a strange way (dad often with his fists). Maybe she had been sent to live with Gran when Maureen was born, but at least she had not been farmed out to a foster family. She had always gone home to eat, and she had never had the slightest doubt about who her dad was.

Myra introduced Ian to her parents and was delighted when he and her father seemed to hit it off so well. However, Nellie didn't like Ian. She was put off by his habit of using big words and long sentences in an effort to appear more intellectual and she didn't trust him, because in some ways he reminded her of her own brutal husband. Love-struck, Myra accused her mother of being prejudiced against Ian because he was from Glasgow – an accusation that Nellie firmly denied. Most of all, there was just something about him that she didn't trust. She didn't think that he would be good for her daughter. Like young women everywhere, Myra didn't give a toss about her mother's opinion of her beau; she was in love and that was really all that mattered.

A Strange Couple

Myra and Ian's relationship soon fell into a routine. They would go to the cinema and then back to Ian's house, where he plied her with wine – generally German wine, because he always favoured all things German – and encouraged her to read the books he liked, and broaden her horizons. Sometimes they brought the books into work, and read them aloud at lunchtime, to the utter bemusement of their co-workers. As well as despising religion, Ian was a racist who believed in Hitler's rants about the Jews and other 'inferior races'.

This was at a time when immigrants from Britain's former colonies, or countries that were still colonies but en route to independence, started to flock to the UK, attracted by the growing economy and the prospect of good jobs and a better life. Most parts of Britain had been almost exclusively white until now; for the first time there were sizeable communities from the West Indies, East Africa and Southeast Asia – Indians and Pakistanis. In this they were perhaps less unusual than in other ways – racism was common at the time and if not accepted, at least generally tolerated. 'No Blacks, No Dogs, No Irish' was a notice still commonly seen in the windows of boarding houses. Nowadays, when someone expresses extreme racist views, alarm bells ring straight away – but that wasn't always the case, and nobody noticed that Ian's views on race were off the charts.

Ian loved Myra's bleached hair, because it reminded him of the German ideal espoused in Hitler's writing. Flattered by this, she vowed never to change it. In fact, she bleached it an even deeper blonde. Ian was fascinated by a woman named Irma Grese, a concentration camp guard who had been executed in 1945 at the age of 22 following her guilty conviction at the Belsen Trial. Myra tried to look as much like Irma as possible. Irma had been known as 'The Beast of Belsen', after the camp she had worked in. She had been infamous at the time for being particularly savage and sadistic with the camp inmates, subjecting them to beatings and shootings, and laughing while they were savaged by the dogs that she kept half-starved for the purpose. A good-looking woman, she had marched about the camp with her blonde hair carefully coiffed, wearing

tailored clothes that suited her rather large, but shapely figure.
For Ian, Myra took great pains with her appearance, wearing dramatic red lipstick and searching out tailored outfits that they thought made her look 'more German', and that suited her Amazonian frame. She kept a photograph of Irma Grese in her handbag so that she would always remember the woman who was supposed to be her inspiration. Myra adopted very short skirts that highlighted her long legs, knee-length boots and leather jackets, all of which made her stand out from the more conservatively dressed Manchester girls. Her new look caused some eyebrows to rise, but the style did suit her.

Ian told Myra that she was different and better than her old friends and neighbours in Gorton, and she lapped it up. She had always wanted to be special and different, and was more than ready to believe Ian's flattery. When she and Ian walked on the streets together, she started ignoring people whom she had known all her life. It was plain to see that her new boyfriend was exerting a powerful influence over her, and that she was not the better for it. People wondered, too, why Myra was affecting a 'posh' accent rather than speaking in her own Mancunian tones. Just who did she think she was? They had all seen her grow up and knew that she was just like them, a scruffy kid whose dad had come home drunk on the weekends, from a home in which there was never quite enough to get by. One of her old friends from school was quoted as saying, 'She went from being this happy-go-lucky girl to not wanting to speak to anybody, not wanting to be with anybody. You'd shout to her and she'd completely ignore you.'

When one of the older members of the staff retired from Millwards Merchandising, Ian received a promotion, and he and Myra worked together much more often. To their mutual satisfaction, her desk was moved next to his. Now they could spend more time together than ever.

Ian had more money now, enough to put down a deposit on a motorbike, on which he sometimes took Myra for a spin. Although Ian was an unreliable boyfriend in many ways, who often stood Myra up when they had arranged to meet, she was besotted with him. In an article published in The Guardian in 1995, she wrote, 'I'd become totally besotted with him, always trying to fathom out the mystery he'd become to me, the aura that emanated from him.'

By now, Myra was a frequent visitor to the library. Her intellect, long neglected, began to blossom as she followed Ian's instructions as to what to read. She took on long and difficult works such as Dostoyevsky's *Crime and Punishment*, a Russian masterpiece that tells the story of a poverty-struck student, Rodion Raskolnikov, who murders a St Petersburg pawnbroker for her money, arguing that he could do good things with the cash, while getting rid of a worthless human being at the same time; the greater good had been accomplished by the killing. Raskolnikov's theory was that not only are some people capable of murder, but that they have the right to commit it. This was a message that Ian was very receptive to, and he liked to expound on it to Myra. *Crime and Punishment* is a very demanding novel that has confounded students of literature to this day. Not bad for a lass from the local Secondary Modern! The girl who had once been put forward with a view of doing the 11-plus, began to come to the fore. Whereas Myra had been put in her place when she failed to make it to grammar school, now she was stretching herself intellectually, and it felt good.

While Ian could be brutal and violent, he was often kind and generous, too. He took Myra out to restaurants and bought her presents every time they had had a disagreement. They had pet names for each other; he referred to her as 'kiddo', or sometimes 'Hess', and she called him Neddie after one of the characters on Ian's beloved Goon Show, which she now professed to love as much as he did. To even the most casual onlooker it seemed that Myra was completely dependent on Ian for everything now; that if he said 'jump', she would simply respond, 'How high'? But others observed that Myra was dominant in many ways. When they went out, for example, she paid for everything, even though Ian – on a bigger salary – provided the funds.

Ian encouraged Myra to learn how to shoot, and she became friendly with the president of a local Rifle Club and visited shooting ranges. George Clitheroe, the president, was surprised to find a young girl so interested in rifles, but helped her to buy a gun from a seller in the city. Myra turned out to be a terrible shot, but nonetheless she bought a number of guns and learned how to take care of, and clean them. She and Ian sometimes fantasised about carrying out a big heist and living an easy life. Myra liked having the guns at home. They must have reminded her of the characters she saw in the films that she and

Ian enjoyed together.

Spicing it Up in Bed

Although Ian was very proud of the intellectual books he liked to read, he also enjoyed the occasional light novel, and made regular forays into popular culture. One piece of light reading that did it for him was The Carpetbaggers, by Harold Robbins, which was published in 1961. With one of the characters allegedly based on the life of Bill Lear, the inventor of the Lear jet, *The Carpetbaggers* was a lurid story set in the south of the United States. The rather flimsy plot was held together by a series of rather explicit sex scenes – at least by the standards of the early 1960s – which were very shocking by the standards of the day, and portrayed wild sex, rape and paedophilia.

The Carpetbaggers had received poor reviews upon publication. In the New York Times it was described as something that should not have been published between the covers of a book, but 'inscribed on the walls of a public lavatory'. The reviewer wrote that the book was, '… an excuse for a collection of monotonous episodes about normal and abnormal sex - and violence ranging from simple battery to gruesome varieties of murder'. All of that made it right up Ian's alley.

The bad review certainly didn't have a negative impact on the book's performance, which had sold over eight million copies by 2004, and has gone down in history as one of the most-read books in the world. The truth was the *The Carpetbaggers* had never pretended to be great literature. It was titillating reading for an audience teetering on the brink of the sexual revolution. Younger readers wanted to show that they weren't the same as their stuffy, conservative parents, and everyone seemed to enjoy the graphic sex scenes. Author Harold Robbins had benefitted greatly from propitious timing – whether deliberately, or by lucky happenstance, we'll never know.

The Carpetbaggers was published at a time when sexual behaviour was on the cusp of dramatic change. The contraceptive pill had been approved for use in the United States in 1960, which meant that for the first time in world history women had access to a reliable form of birth control. Until only recently, books of considerable literary merit, such as DH Lawrence's *Lady Chatterley's Lover* had been banned in many countries for their sexually explicit content. This, of course, only served to make them even more popular. When it came to sex, it seemed that the younger generation simply couldn't get enough.

Like millions of other readers, Ian Brady loved The Carpetbagger's and was titillated by the sex scenes it portrayed so vividly. He showed the book to Myra, and told her that it showed that rape, incest and paedophilia were fun adventures that maybe, just maybe, they could engage in – or at least fantasise about. Who cared if people got hurt along the way? Some individuals were special, and stood apart from everyone else. They had the right to take what they wanted from life, even when that meant trampling on others.

As they grew closer and closer, Ian began to share more of his violent sexual fantasies with his girlfriend, who had already shown herself to be more than prepared to join in. He had found violence attractive from puberty, and while his friends had sniggered at the girly pictures that they bought and passed around, the very tame pornography available in the 1950s had never been enough for Ian. He wanted the real thing, and he wanted it hard, fast and furious. Pornography and dirty books never went as far as the exciting scenarios he ran through in his own head. Myra had already posed for numerous saucy pictures for her beloved. When he asked her to go farther, she was able and willing to oblige. Her experience of sex so far had given her a taste for violence. In a frenzied lovemaking session, Ian bit Myra all over her body until her white skin was covered in dark bruises, and then photographed her in a suggestive pose that he could enjoy later. She lapped it all up.

To make their sex life more adventurous, Ian persuaded Myra to take part in sex games based on scenes from the novel, and apparently she was more than willing to oblige. She enjoyed dressing up and getting Ian excited, and the challenge of getting into character for one of their romps. By now, Ian was spending many nights at Myra's house. If her Gran objected, perhaps she was by now too elderly to make her complaints heard. One hopes that she was too deaf by then to hear the groans and screeches that must have emanated from the rutting pair.

Rather more intellectual than The Carpetbaggers, but still focused on the darker side of sex, Myra and Ian were also inspired by the work of the Marquis de Sade, whose writing Ian had often boasted about enjoying. De Sade's work, much of which was written in the various asylums and prisons in which he spent so much of his life throughout the eighteenth century, combined philosophy with raunchy, violent sexual fantasies and blasphemy. Apparently Ian sometimes asked Myra to get de Sade books for him from the library. He would become aroused while reading them, after which he would beat her and have rough sex.

Despite having an active sex life with Myra, Ian showed some homosexual tendencies. He had told her quite openly that he liked to go to a number of local pubs that were well known as a meeting place for homosexual men. While Myra never knew exactly what Ian got up to there, apparently she accepted these unconventional leanings as part of the complex whole that he was. Later, Myra wrote frankly about their sex life, describing some of the rather ritualistic scenes they enacted in their lovemaking:

Ian took the lead most times. He enjoyed rough sex and light spankings became whippings... He excited me in a way that no other man had done before... I needed to drink to perform for him or to do the things Ian wanted to do. He liked me to dress up like a tart, for us both to wear hoods. He enjoyed anal sex the most... he also enjoyed having a candle inserted up his backside. It gave us both pleasure, especially me, because then I was in the dominant role.

Ian had been working at Millwards Merchandising for more than three years by this stage. He had not progressed very far, by his own reckoning, and had grown resentful about his place in the world. He was fed up of being part of the working classes, when a man of his inestimable talents should have risen much farther by now.

He didn't want to live in the grimy streets of a run-down area. That wasn't good enough for him. He deserved and needed a gracious home and a rewarding career. The world was full of scumbags, working-class oafs, and racially inferior immigrants who didn't deserve success. He was special. He needed more. Myra agreed with him. Life wasn't fair. Why were they stuck in the rough end of Manchester when there was so much to discover out there? Why were other people living in big houses and drinking fancy, expensive wine, when they had to make do with what they could afford?

Violence Spills Over from Fantasy to Real Life

As time passed, Ian and Myra's taste for violence grew until they wanted a taste of the real thing. Myra had a pet dog, Puppet, and loved animals, and although Ian had previously been cruel to animals, he now targeted those convicted of animal cruelty. They started out by focusing on locals, and simply went to these offenders' houses, and threw a brick through their window to give them a lesson, but when possible, Ian would beat them up. They bonded closely over their exploits, which made them feel as though they were standing up for the defenceless, like fearless vigilantes. Ian saw animals as superior to people in many ways, as did Myra, who had a particular fondness for dogs. They felt completely justified in their violent actions towards anyone who mistreated a harmless pet.

Then Ian came across another book that spoke to him. Written by Meyer Levin and published in 1956, Compulsion was based on the real-life story about Nathan Leopold and Richard Loeb, students at the University of Chicago who had kidnapped and murdered a fourteen year-old boy called Bobby Franks, in 1924. Their only reason for doing so was to commit the perfect crime. Like Ian, Leopold and Loeb were huge fans of the German philosopher Nietzsche. Nietzsche had written about the ideal man, or 'Superman' and they felt that they were supermen, and that therefore the ordinary rules did not apply to them. Once again, this was a message that Ian felt applied to him, too.

Leopold and Loeb planned the kidnapping and murder for months, choosing Bobby because he was the son of a Chicago millionaire. Shortly after the kidnapping, the young boy was murdered. He may or may not have been sexually assaulted – in those days forensic science was not very evolved, and apparently there was no conclusive evidence either way. After disfiguring the body with hydrochloric acid, it was hidden, and a ransom note sent to the family.

Despite their careful planning, the pair were quickly apprehended, as Leopold had lost a pair of very distinctive glasses at the scene of the body's disposal, and the police were able to trace him. They confessed quite quickly, and admitted that their main aim in killing young Bobby had simply been the thrill.

The blurb on the back of the book read, 'You know why we did it? Because we damn well felt like doing it!'

This was a book that could have been written for Ian. He pored over it and was astounded by how stupidly the kidnapping and murder had been carried out. They had done everything wrong. As Ian saw it, their biggest mistake had been their appalling lack of planning.

Ian told Myra that if they were to commit the perfect murder, they would never make so many stupid mistakes. They would put in time to plan properly.

It had become clear that Ian was now ready to move away from fantasy and take a giant step towards really carrying out the awful deeds that he often talked about.

According to Myra, things had now gone so far that she literally felt unable to step away. Writing about this time later, she stated:

He began to talk about the perfect murder, and I thought that, too, was another fantasy. But one night he asked me if I wanted to see anyone I didn't like dead. I said no, I didn't dislike anyone that much...

Then one evening - and he hadn't been drinking - he told me he wanted to do a perfect murder and I was going to help him.

I knew by the time he began talking about the perfect murder that I was going to help him, that I had very little choice. Again, even if I went to the police there was no proof, only my word against his. And then he would know what I'd done if the police had told him I'd made these allegations against him, and although I knew he wasn't stupid enough to do anything to draw attention to himself, I also knew that he would bide his time while he thought of what to do and how to do it without raising suspicion.

I would have had to leave my job, which wasn't a problem; I could go away and lose myself somewhere, but how could I possibly tell my family all that had happened and been said by him without terrifying them?

They couldn't move; a family just can't uproot itself and move somewhere and find places to live, jobs etc; and still live in fear, looking over their shoulders all the time. I knew I was trapped and would have to do what he wanted of me.

This was a pivotal moment in Ian and Myra's relationship, and one that would have fatal consequences. Ian and Myra were about to move from fantasy to reality. Years later, when she made a plea for parole to the then Home Secretary, Merlyn Rees, Myra wrote:

Within months he [Brady] had convinced me that there was no God at all: he could have told me that the earth was flat, the moon was made of green cheese and the sun rose in the west, I would have believed him, such was his power of persuasion.

The truth, however, is that Myra had been a willing participant in every single one of Ian's sick games, every step of the way, and now she was prepared to go the extra mile.

The more they read and thought about the perfect murder, the more convinced Ian and Myra became that they would be capable of carrying one out. They had already determined that they were far superior to everyone else. While most of the people they knew read just trashy romances and tabloid newspapers, they pored over intellectual books and poetry, and tried to get inside the mind of some of the world's most influential thinkers, like Nietzsche and Hitler. They had studied the crimes of people like them, who had wanted to kill just because it was fun, and because some people had a right to do it – but unlike them, they would plan carefully and carry out their crimes meticulously. They would do it properly, and they would not be caught.

They were special. They weren't like other people. They had retreated so deeply inside their fantasy world that the lies they were telling themselves seemed to make perfect sense.

And that is when the killing started.

Rather more intellectual than The Carpetbaggers, but still focused on the darker side of sex, Myra and Ian were also inspired by the work of the Marquis de Sade, whose writing Ian had often boasted about enjoying. De Sade's work, much of which was written in the various insane asylums and prisons in which he spent so much of his life throughout the eighteenth century, combined philosophy with raunchy, violent sexual fantasies and blasphemy. Apparently Ian sometimes asked Myra to get de Sade books for him from the library. He would become aroused while reading them, after which he would beat her and have rough sex.

Chapter 5

Saddleworth Moor

Saddleworth Moor

Once at the Moors, Brady arrived behind them, and Hindley introduced him as her boyfriend, who would help them find the glove. Hindley's story says that Pauline went alone into the Moors with Brady, who did not return for around 30 minutes or more, and then he guided Hindley back to the dying Pauline, her throat cut, her clothing in disarray. Hindley said that Brady then ordered her to watch the girl while Brady went to fetch the spade to dig her grave. It was later said that Hindley was there all along, including being the actual person to smash the girl's head with the spade and contribute to the rape. When the story was repeated to officials, Hindley shared that they had passed Pauline's mother and brother searching for Pauline on their way home that night.

Saddleworth Moor is located in South Pennines of Northern England, and is named for a parish to its south. The land is located in the Peak District National Park, specifically the higher and wilder area of Dark Peak that has a layer of limestone covered by Millstone Grit and is mostly uninhabited. Much like a bog in many areas, the landscape includes valleys, fast flowing streams, drainage channels, and some scattered farmsteads. There is road access such as A635, also known as the Isle of Skye Road. Some people, including Ian Brady, enjoyed Saddleworth Moor and visited it often as a place for gatherings, picnics, and walks.

The Moors Murders were so named because of the location of the bodies in Saddleworth Moor, which was towards Dovestones Reservoir, and is located in Saddleworth, Greater Manchester.

Though many sections of the Moors have names given to them by local visitors, sections of the Moors identified during the searches included an area southwest of Broadstone Hill, between Hollin Brown Knoll and Greenfield Reservoir. The three shallow graves found were located off A635 road, and each was a location featured in Brady and Hindley's photographs. The couple had numerous photographs of the Moors, and locating which ones identified gravesites had been difficult, but also more so because matching them to the exact locations had been challenging. The difficulty was particularly noticeable in the search for the final missing boy's body, which resulted in searchers examining areas between Hollin Brown Knoll and Wessenden Moor, particularly along the Shiny Brook before it reaches Wessenden Reservoir.

Ian Brady expressed a great love for Saddleworth Moors, making numerous trips to the location and even taking many different photographs at different places in the moors. The photos were sometimes nearly documentarian in nature, pictures of the scenery throughout the Moors, seemingly with no other intention than to capture a moment in time. Other pictures were of Myra and her puppy, Puppet. Still more were of Ian and Myra smiling for the camera, or one or the other alone in the chilly weather of Saddleworth Moors. Locations of the photographs included the beautiful Ramshaw Rocks, Oldham, Broadstone Hill, Middle Edge Moss, and Hollin Brown Knoll. Police and campaigners worked diligently to use the photographs to try to decipher where Keith Bennett's body had been buried, but to no avail. Hindley and Brady were eventually able to bring legal action to have all their photographs returned to them, with only the exception of the ones that police were able to identify as evidence for the crimes. Many different individuals have reviewed the images, however, Hindley had the other photographs sent to her mother for safekeeping and some people believe that they may still hold more evidence within them. To date, no significant progress has been made using the remaining photographs, though some supposition has been gained.

Brady's interest in the Moors began as a young child, when his adoptive parents took him there for a short visit. He wandered up on a small hill, away from the family while they were sleeping. When they awoke, they saw him off in the distance, standing staring into the horizon, away from them, and he would say that he felt empowered there, on that hill silhouetted against the sky. Later, he would stress that for those moments he truly understood himself, especially his endless desire to be alone. Somehow he believed that place understood him, and for as far as you could see, the landscape was quiet, even if at times unwelcoming, which he expressed as understanding of his inner self. His fascination was not only a childhood revelation, but also an obsession, and as an adult, he and Myra Hindley would later live in a home where they could overlook the Moors. The bodies of three of their victims were found in the northernmost tip of the Peak District National Park, which is known as a barren area of the Saddleworth Moors, mostly made up of grassy moorland with deep valleys, fast flowing streams, peat, coarse-grained sandstone, and millstone grit. It is unknown if Brady and Hindley laid their victims in these shallow graves to give themselves trophies in their home away from home, or to provide the land with something to fill the emptiness of the place itself.

Brady and Hindley did not always go alone to the Moors, but often visited with family and friends. Brady had such a love for the place that he went many times a week, including for holidays and casual picnics, bringing along visitors to share in the experiences. They visited often with David Smith, who they later tried to involve in their crimes. David Smith was the husband of Hindley's sister, Maureen, and the couple joined Hindley and Brady on numerous drunken trips through the Moors, exploring or just drinking lazily in one of the many scenic areas. Later, after the death of Edward Evans, Brady would admit to Smith that bodies of his earlier victims were buried in the Moors, and this would eventually lead to numerous searches and eventually, the bodies. The Moors were valuable to Brady and Hindley, and they shared this interest with everyone willing to visit it with them, especially in autumn, which was Brady's favourite time of year.

At this time, in 1964, the couple lived in Hindley's grandmother's house located in Hattersley council estate. They spent a great deal of time with Hindley's sister and her husband, David Smith. Brady was impressed with the young man, and enjoyed beguiling him with his personal beliefs.

Another person who visited the Moors with them was a young girl called Patricia Ann Hodges. At the time of Patricia's friendship with Brady and Hindley, she was barely eleven years old, and lived two doors down from the couple. She was part of a very large family of seven children, and visited the couple often. They even had a photograph of her with them in their home.

Many people believe that Patricia was one of the luckiest children of that time, because while Brady and Hindley spent a great deal of time with her, including sharing alcohol with her (wine, whisky and gin), and visiting the Moors, the couple never sexually abused or killed Patty, as Hindley referred to her. The young girl even went as often as a few times a week to the Moors with the couple, unaware of the danger she could have been in during her visits. On more than one occasion, it seemed they brought her to a place where they would later bury a body, or they had already buried one. She also went alone for walks with one or the other at different times.

Patricia had been in grave danger quite a few times, that she had not been aware of during her visits. They even had recorded her reading the local newspaper, specifically the articles regarding the disappearances of Lesley Ann Downey and John Kilbride, though this incident occurred without the girl's knowledge of the recording. This particular orchestrated moment most clearly demonstrates how fortunate she was not to have become another of the Moors murders. Another time of concern occurred one Christmas, when Hindley and Brady took her to the Moors, intent on spending the night there; however, she was returned home in the early hours at 1:30 am. It was the very next day that the couple would kidnap Leslie Ann Downey. Later, when asked about Patricia, Hindley would insist that there were never any ill intentions towards Patty, and that her relationship with the girl was purely innocent, and not interfered with by Brady. As an adult, Patricia still thought of those times, amazed to still be alive, and pained that she had known such vicious killers.

Pauline Reade

Pauline Reade was sixteen years old and a friend of Myra Hindley's sister, Maureen, and a nearby neighbour to Brady and Hindley. Born on 18 February 1947, she lived with her parents, father Amos, mother Joan and her brother Paul, at 9 Wiles Street in Gorton. The family was very close and enjoyed each other's company. People who knew Pauline described her as shy, pretty, and slim. She was always hardworking and dedicated to her causes. She had dark hair and bright blue eyes that shone when she worked with her father, training to become a baker at Sharples, on Cross Lane. Every day she would spend her early mornings working there alongside her father, and learning the trade so that she, too, could be a baker. Her talent was growing with the nurturing guidance from her father, and during the Christmas cake competition, in 1962, Pauline had been one of three winners for a cake she had made herself. Her success was featured in the Gorton Reporter, and was a matter of pride for her family, and many of her friends were inspired by her success. She was never prideful, or made others feel less important.

Pauline was a typical teenage girl in her interests and activities, and was described as affectionate and loving by her family. Similar to other teenagers during the times, she had a passion for dancing that was her very inspiration, and she often involved her friends in this interest. Her father had taken her to a dinner dance in London, which was something that she was quite fond of, entrancing and powering her desire to dance even further. She already spent her free time writing poems and songs, and learning to play the piano. Pauline and her father often played the piano together. Her love for music and dance was a guiding influence in her life, but it was also what led to her being out during that fateful night.

Many of Pauline's closest friends lived in her neighbourhood, and were children her age who also enjoyed dance and music. The other teenagers and neighbours described her as softly spoken, not the type of girl who would get into a car with strangers. Most people who knew her well also noted that she was very supportive and protective of her friends and family. Though little else is known about Pauline Reade, specifically in regards to what she knew of or thought of Hindley, it is unlikely that she would have got into the vehicle with Hindley if she had not known her already. Hindley was Maureen's older sister and lived near Pauline's home, and while the girls were not close, Pauline was generally a helpful girl and would not have denied assistance to a woman she knew.

On 12 July 1963, Pauline was on her way to go dancing at the British Railways Club. Brady and Hindley had already passed another potential victim for their perfect crime when they took a different route that brought them to Pauline. Her path took her down Froxmer Street, and it was there that Brady spotted her from his motorbike, in her party dress of pink and gold, blue coat and white high-heeled shoes. Having already worked out the code with Hindley, he signalled her to stop and approached the teenage girl. Under the pretense of needing help to find a very expensive glove, Hindley convinced Pauline to get into the van and go with her to the Moors. Pauline did not mind, saying that she had plenty of time before she had to be at the dance, and was willing to help, as she recognized Myra Hindley as Maureen's sister. Brady followed them to the Moors on his motorbike.

Once at the Moors, Brady arrived behind them, and Hindley introduced him as her boyfriend, who would help them find the glove. Hindley's story says that Pauline went alone into the Moors with Brady, who did not return for around 30 minutes or more, and then he guided Hindley back to the dying Pauline, her throat cut, her clothing in disarray. Hindley said that Brady then ordered her to watch the girl while Brady went to fetch the spade to dig her grave. It was later said that Hindley was there all along, including being the actual person to smash the girl's head with the spade and contribute to the rape. When the story was repeated to officials, Hindley shared that they had passed Pauline's mother and brother searching for Pauline on their way home that night.

Though this was the very first murder committed by the couple, Pauline's body would be the last to be found (excluding the still missing body of Keith Bennett). Hindley would lead police in their search after confessing to knowledge of both Pauline's and Keith's murders. Though it is believed that she confessed only due to her concern that Brady's mental condition and possible confession would be poor publicity for herself, it may have also been in direct relation to the letters from Keith Bennett's mother, though most people do not believe that alone would have encouraged a confession. Later, it was suggested that Hindley's cooperation was only to garner support for one her many attempts to have her sentence reduced. Neither Hindley nor Brady uncovered the body, both claiming that they could not locate the bodies due to the changes in Saddleworth Moors in the many years since their visits. However, most people felt that both were simply seeking media attention, with Hindley wanting more evidence to suggest she had been reformed and should be released. At no time were her confessions or assistance enough to sway the strict sentence of life that was afforded her for her crimes.

Pauline's body was found in 1987, nearly twenty-four years after her death on July 12th. Her body was located not far from Lesley Ann Downey's body, and closer to Broadstone Hill than the A635 road. While Pauline's mother had been at the site, she was not present during the discovery of the body in the 91.4 cm grave. It was a place that would have easily been seen from Hollin Brown Knoll, just as described by Hindley in her efforts to assist with the search. This direction from Hindley was the guiding aspect to locating the body, rather than the pictures themselves, which were used as grave markers. When her body was found, it was reportedly well preserved in peat, and her clothing was still intact; however, there was no way to determine if she had been sexually assaulted. Even in its preservation, her body was difficult to recognize due to the many years it had rested in the ground; her clothes were the first clue that it was she, and further examination confirmed the identity. Her cause of death is believed to be the direct result of the beating about the head and shoulders, or the violent slash across her throat that was so deep it severed the spinal cord. Brady and Hindley were not prosecuted for the death of Pauline Reade because they were already serving life sentences for the other murders. Pauline Reade was a beautiful young girl with a bright future who was violently deprived of life by the Moors murderers.

John Kilbride

John Kilbride was aged twelve at the time of his abduction and murder, which occurred four months after the first murder. Kilbride was one of five children, and known to many in his neighbourhood and by many schoolmates. He had gone off that particular day, without his siblings, to try to earn pocket money by helping out in the nearby market. Hindley and Brady met Kilbride while he was at the market helping stall-holders, in Ashton-under-Lyne, during the evening of 23 November 1963. When the boy was selected, Hindley approached the boy alone, at first asking for help with her boxes. The boy was then told that his parents would be worried about him, because it was getting late, and that Hindley and Brady could drive him home. To further garner the boy's trust and willingness to join them, they offered to share with him a bottle of sherry before taking him to his house, and to this the boy agreed. However, obtaining the sherry required that they stop by their home where they had left the bottle. They did not return to the home of Hindley and Brady, but instead stopped by the Moors.

They stopped at the Moors to supposedly look for an expensive lost glove of Hindley's. Upon reaching the Moors, both Kilbride and Brady got out to look for the glove, and according to Hindley, she remained in the vehicle under the pretense of locking up. The vehicle was a Ford Anglia she had hired. According to Hindley, Brady sexually assaulted Kilbride and then killed the boy, and Hindley claimed not to have witnessed any of this crime. Brady was unsuccessful in slicing the boy's throat, due to the attempted use of a serrated knife, killing him instead by strangling him with a piece of string, which may have been a shoelace. Brady then buried Kilbride and the couple returned to their home. This location would also be documented with a photograph that would guide police to the shallow grave.

Kilbride's disappearance did not have as much notice as it might have done because it occurred the day after the murder of President Kennedy in the United States, but his body was one of the first bodies located during the searches. Photographs of the Moors were the mementos of these two murders, and Hindley was posed at the grave of this boy with her dog, Puppet. This enabled the police to locate him during their searches. Kilbride's body was located off the A635 road, an area that could be overlooked by Hollin Brown Knoll, but was across the road towards the Greenfield Reservoir. Evidence of the sexual assault was in his jeans and underpants tangled about his thighs, and knotted in the back. Of the three bodies located, his was the only one located on the side towards Middle Edge Moss; however, other photographs were taken in those areas.

Over the past 50 years, John's siblings, especially Danny, spoke out that life should mean life for the paedophile killers, and worked towards preventing the release of Brady and Hindley. In 2011, John's younger brother Danny lost his battle with cancer, and was survived by their siblings Patrick, Terry, Sheila, and Maria. The struggle with the events around John Kilbride's disappearance was difficult for their family, and eventually it caused their parents to separate. Over the years, Danny had been the spokesperson for the entire family, and though he would not leave it to time, he was not obsessed, only determined in his commitment. His family of six children, and wife Anne, described him as loving and jolly in nature, filled with humour and compassion. The remaining siblings have told reporters their one wish is that people will remember John, and they feel that wish continues to be true, especially with people who went to school with the family and with John.

Keith Bennett

Keith Bennett lived on Eston Street with his mother, stepfather (Winnie and Jimmy Johnson), his two brothers, and two sisters. The oldest of the children, Keith was often afforded a great deal of respect from the younger siblings, and enabled him to walk much of the distance to his grandmother's house alone. The Bennett children were close to their aunt and grandmother, who lived just a short distance from their home. It was common for the children to walk to their house for visits. Their mother worked at the Electricity Board on Bax Road, which left the children to spend their time in the local baths. Keith excelled at swimming, and worked to teach his younger siblings how to swim during their free hours while their mother was at work. After work, their mother would stop by and fetch them to walk home.

One brother's fondest memories, was of Keith's attempts to teach him to swim, and while he remembers he didn't like it, he says it was Keith's greatest skill. Like the other children that Hindley and Brady preyed upon, Keith Bennett was much loved by his family for his generosity towards his family, and his great love of life. Many people described Keith as a happy boy with a tendency to daydream that negatively influenced his success in school, but endeared him to many people. He was often admiring nature and had been very unhappy when their pet tortoise died, even to the extent that he believed the tortoise might not have been dead during its burial. The family was close, and Keith is remembered as a good older brother to the children. Many people, from family members to schoolmates, often wonder what he would have been like as an adult, what type of career he would have chosen, and how he would have been as a father.

On 16 June 1964, twelve-year-old Keith Bennett was on his way to his grandmother's house when Brady and Hindley abducted him. The couple were driving in Chorlton-on-Medlock in Manchester when they approached Keith. Hindley was able to convince the boy to get into her vehicle, a mini-pick-up, by asking for his help to move some boxes and offering him a ride home after. The couple took Keith to a lay-by at the Moors where Hindley said Brady went off with the boy on the pretence of looking for her missing glove. When he returned, he told her he had sexually assaulted the boy, and strangled him with a piece of string. Later the story would change, and it would suggest that Hindley had indeed been watching as Brady sexually assaulted the boy in a ravine, prior to strangling him. Hindley reportedly destroyed the photograph memento evidence of this crime, while at Brady's work during the time between his arrest and hers. Had this not occured, the photographs may have guided police to Keith's body.

It was November 1986 when Brady admitted to the murders of Keith Bennett and Pauline Reade, only after Hindley had admitted to the crimes, though possibly to a reporter prior to that event. Both Hindley and Brady would claim they wanted to help locate the bodies, but none of the three trips taken between them turned up the Bennett boy. The couple did not provide any sufficient direction, other than the lead to the location of Pauline's body. Over the years, the police have searched many locations, and have been reluctant to put any more effort into the hunt without sufficient evidence to warrant new digs. Numerous people over the years have suggested possible locations, and privately funded hunts have occurred. The family currently manages a website intended to inform people about the young boy who went missing and to provide updated information regarding the hunt for his body.

The body of Keith Bennett has never been found, but some people believe him to have been buried near Ramshaw Rocks, in Staffordshire, due to a photograph of Brady holding a puppy in that location. Other campaigners believe they have located the place of Bennett's burial, due to a spade having been found near a location Brady had described previously, that of two waterfalls, and stone-walled sheep pens. Brady himself had felt too disorientated to locate the exact spot when he was taken to guide the search in 1987, partially because the sheep pens had moved. However, the recent rusted spade has not resulted in continuing searches for the boy's body. Police do not feel that sufficient information or evidence supports another search of that location. Numerous people have stated that Brady has shared with police that he was in the habit of breaking the shovels and leaving the spade (later disposing of the handle such as by burning) in order to reduce the likelihood that the police could trace it back to the murder. In addition, people who believe the spade to be a significant find, point out that the location is significant, in that neither the Ramshaw Rocks location, nor this location have been identified for continued searching by the police. However, campaigners continue to diligently seek out the location of Keith Bennett.

In addition to campaigners and researchers seeking out the location of Keith Bennett, some people believe that Brady has supplied the correct and complete information to the body in a letter he wrote to Bennett's mother. The letter and an autobiography are scheduled for release upon Brady's death; however, Winnie Johnson (Bennett's mother) has since passed away. Alan Bennett, Keith's brother, continues to petition for assistance with the case, but the case was formally closed, and may not be opened again without new evidence. Many people believe that Brady does not know where the body is, but continues to use it to garner attention from the press and from police. Other people believe that it is his last opportunity to remain in control, and that he withholds the information to demonstrate his control.

Lesley Ann Downey

The fourth victim of the evil couple was a ten-year-old girl named Lesley Ann Downey. Lesley Ann was the only girl in her family, and for that very Christmas, she had received a sewing machine to learn how to make clothing for her dolls. Her brother Terry would later tell reporters that she herself was often referred to as a doll, their little porcelain doll – innocent, with dark curly tresses and apple cheeks. Her family remembered the young girl as helpful and friendly, eager to work with her mother, and talk with her stepfather and brother. This particular description was the one that best describes a portrait of the young girl; Terry West told reporters that was how he most remembered his little sister.

Lesley Ann was picked up at the fairground in Ancoats, the day after Christmas in 1964. Her helpful nature made her an easy target for the couple, as the young girl helped pick up boxes when Hindley had dropped them (purposefully) in front of her. They convinced her to assist in carrying packages to their car, and to go back to their home to take the boxes out of the car. Once at the house, she was forcibly undressed, gagged, photographed, raped, and strangled, though which abuses were done by Brady or Hindley, remain unclear; the police found the photographs and a voice tape of the interactions. According to Brady, Hindley had been the one to kill Lesley Ann. After killing the child, she was put into a shallow grave with her clothing at her feet.

Her screams and pleas were a devastating contrast to the soft Christmas carols playing during a 16 minute, 21 second tape. This particular evidence was horrifying for all listeners, as it clearly demonstrated the desperation and fear of the girl as she begged for her life, for her mother, and even for God. Her pleas were completely ignored by her captors, other than for them to ask her not to be so loud and to do as they asked. Later in court, Hindley would claim innocence, having only been involved with the photographs, and claiming to be in the other room running a bath for Lesley Ann at the time of the sexual assault and the murder. However, during cross-examination, Brady stated, 'then we all got dressed' during his description of the events leading up to Lesley Ann's death. This particular remark suggested that Hindley, too, was involved in at least the sexual molestation of the child.

Ann West never stopped hating Hindley and Brady for their atrocities and the torture of her young and innocent daughter, and the family would suffer many years to come after Lesley Ann's death. The knowledge that Hindley was aware of the abuse to her daughter, and the belief that Hindley had also molested her daughter, made Ann West swear that if she were ever released from prison, she herself would kill Hindley for her crimes. Ann West worked her entire life to ensure that Hindley never left prison, even after a seven-page letter Hindley wrote. The severe hatred of Hindley, led West and her family to wish death upon the two murderers, and they were successful in preventing Hindley's release, though Ann died in 1999, three years before Hindley.

Edward Evans

The oldest of the victims, at age seventeen, was Edward Evans. He was an apprentice engineer. This murder would lead to their arrest, making this particular incident essential to the case, and the only thing that prevented them from killing unknown numbers of more children. Edward was believed to be homosexual, which made him a target, particularly for Brady, but the downfall was his interest in sharing his crimes with David Smith, Hindley's brother-in-law. David Smith would be a witness to Edward's murder, and forced to assist in the moving of the boy's body, though not a contributor to the murder itself.

Edward was selected by Brady at the Manchester Central Station, where Hindley said she waited in the car for him to return with his chosen victim. The story is that Brady was able to attract the attention of the young man by offering him casual sex. Brady then brought Edward to Hindley, who he said was his sister, and proceeded to take him home. Once back at their house, Brady and Edward were in the living room and the three enjoyed a bottle of wine while relaxing. After the wine, Brady quietly sent Hindley to bring back her brother-in-law, David Smith. Brady hoped to involve Smith in the murder of the young man, and believed that he would require help to move the body, as he would be too heavy for Hindley to help with after the murder.

According to Hindley, the relationship between Smith and Brady had become compromised, and this particular incident proved exactly that. She went out and called for Smith, asking him to come over and help her. She explained to Smith that Brady wanted to give him some miniature wine bottles, and that he should stop over to get them. Brady believed that Smith would be a willing participant due to his history with crime, and his willingness to repeat the ideology that Brady told him was true and accurate. Edwards was believed to have engaged in sexual activities with Brady during the time between when Hindley left to get Smith, and Smith's entrance into the house.

Upon returning home, she made Smith wait outside until she gave him a signal. The sign was a flashing light, and Smith knocked on the door, resulting in Brady answering the door and asking loudly if he had come for the miniature wine bottles. Following this, Brady left Smith in the kitchen under the pretense of collecting the bottles. Shortly after, Smith heard a scream, and Hindley shouted for help; Smith hurried into the living room to discover Brady hitting Evans with the an axe, the flat end, and then strangling the boy with an electrical cord. Brady had hurt his ankle during the altercation, and therefore could not move the body alone, so Smith and Brady wrapped it, and stored it in the spare bedroom to be taken to the Moors, which Smith had agreed to help with, promising to come by the next evening. Edward Evans died in October 1965, and David Smith put an end to the Moors Murders with the help of his wife and the local police.

Many people believe that Patricia was one of the luckiest children of that time, because while Brady and Hindley spent a great deal of time with her, including sharing alcohol with her (wine, whisky, and gin), and visiting the Moors, the couple never sexually abused or killed Patty, as Hindley referred to her. The young girl even went as often as a few times a week to the Moors with the couple, unaware of the danger she could have been in during her visits. On more than one occasion, it seemed they brought her to a place where they would later bury a body, or they had already buried one. She also went alone for walks with one or the other at different times.

Chapter 6

David Smith Blows the Cover

David Smith Blows the Cover

Realising for the first time that he was really face to face with genuine evil, David was absolutely terrified. If Ian had killed all those people, as he had just killed Eddie, what was stopping him from doing David in, too? Eddie had been seventeen years old; David was seventeen as well. Eddie had been no match for the ruthless Ian, and David knew that if push came to shove, he wouldn't be either. Most of all, David knew that if Ian thought that he might shop him to the police, he wouldn't stand a chance. There was no way Ian was going to let himself be taken by the coppers.

David knew that if he didn't do exactly as Ian said, he could easily be next. Ian wouldn't give a toss about the fact that he was Myra's brother-in-law, and David had no reason to suppose that Myra would be any more sympathetic. Their masks had slipped and he had seen them both for the villains that they were.

David Smith

Hailed by many as the man who stopped the Moors Murders, David Smith has suffered a number of challenges since that fateful day when he was forced to witness the brutal murder of Edward Evans. At the young age of 17, much of the public accused him of contributing to the murders due to claims by Hindley and Brady that he was an accessory to or had committed the murders that they were charged with as part of the Moor's Murders. David's life would continue to be a challenge until his death in May 2012. No moment in his life was untouched by the horrific things he witnessed in 1965 or the experiences that followed. Though his family described him as a loving man who was a hero, having saved the world from more lost and abused children, others believed him an escaped murderer and were cruel to his family, including his children.

David Smith was the brother-in-law of Myra Hindley, having married her younger sister Maureen when she discovered she was pregnant. He was a young man with a difficult history of rebellion and disobedience. The few years that David knew Myra Hindley were years that she was in a relationship with Ian Brady. Those years would change his entire life, not only would they be the beginning of his life, as a parent, but those years would change how he viewed the world around him and how it viewed him. In just a few hours, everything would change for the young man, and for decades, it was not for the better.

Into the Family

On January 9, 1948, in south Manchester, David Smith was born to an unmarried teenage mother by the name of Joyce Hull. His mother did not stay with him and he would never meet her, but his father Jack Smith ensured that he would be cared for by placing him with his own parents, who later adopted David as their own son. Later, aged 6, David would join Jack in Gorton; however, life heading into his teens was troubled and he was already having difficulty with other students and authority. Aged 11, he was expelled from Stanley Grove secondary school for punching a headmaster at the school. During that same year, he would be required to appear in court for using a knife on a boy during a fight. At the very next school, David would be removed from the school for using a cricket bat on a boy during another fight, and sent to Rose Hill Remand Home at Northenden. From there, he went to school at St. James's Secondary Modern in Gorton. He soon left to begin his adult life.

David's past made him an easy choice of Brady's; he demonstrated a background that suggested he might be a good new recruit to his growing plans to commit atrocities and crimes. Myra Hindley was not always strong enough to assist with the activities, and David was a strong young man. His introduction to Brady was a direct result of his relationship with Maureen Hindley. Maureen and David met at St. James' School in Gorton and began seeing each other regularly. Smith had difficulty in school, though not all his difficulty was behavioural in nature, he had begun to lose interest in learning and responsibility. Maureen was already a factory machinist, and then David left the school to take a job as an apprentice electrician, a position his father helped him obtain. At this young age, he was unable to handle the responsibilities and was often late for work, causing him to lose the job. He then began to do odd jobs around the local area. While David was doing odd jobs, in 1964, Maureen discovered she was pregnant and the two got married in August of that same year. They were unable to honeymoon, but Brady and Myra gave them a wedding present. The present was a trip to the Lake District, which Brady and Hindley happily drove them to on the day after their wedding.

While Brady and Myra had given them a nice wedding present, they weren't overly friendly to begin with. When they first met, David did not have many feelings or thoughts about Myra or Brady, who seemed to be distant from the rest of the family and rarely involved with their lives. David even described Brady as just the Scotsman and Myra as an unsmiling hard person. When Maureen gave birth to their daughter, Angela, David thought life would be a typical family life, but at six months, Angela died of cot death. Maureen and David were devastated, but they arranged a funeral with the help of the family. For the funeral, Myra brought them a card and flowers, the gesture seemed sincere and appropriate. Brady had not attended the funeral himself, but sat instead in the car smoking. After the funeral, Myra and Brady began spending more time with them. They went up to the Moors together with bottles of wine and sometimes the guns for shooting. The friendship with Brady and Hindley was fuelled by the availability of alcohol, a vehicle, and the older couple's money.

In addition, David did feel comfortable around them in the beginning, encouraged by the fact that Brady too had teenage difficulties with the law. In addition, David was young enough to still be impressed with Brady's three-piece suits, his sophisticated mannerisms, and his ability to play chess. Some changes in his views of Brady came from his rhetoric, which was often not something David was amicable with; he was willing to overlook these things for the sake of the friendship and the family. Even the vies of Nazism and the strange discussions regarding the legitimacy of rape and murder. However, less than a week before the murder of Edward

Visitors to the burial site of 10-year-old murder victim Lesley Ann
Downey on Saddleworth Moor in the South Pennines, 1965.

Mrs Ann Downey (later West) watching the police search Saddleworth Moor for the body of her daughter Lesley, a victim of the Moors Murderers Ian Brady and Myra Hindley, 18th October 1965.

Police search Saddleworth Moor around the spot where a second body was found, 21st October 1965.

Police digging up the back garden of Ian Brady's house in Wardle Brook Avenue, Hattersley, 24th October 1965.

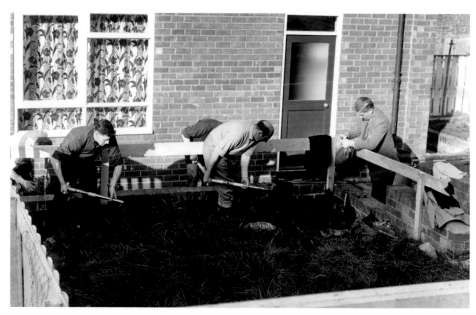

Police digging up the back garden of Ian Brady's house in Wardle Brook Avenue, Hattersley, 26th October 1965.

Ian Brady's house in Wardle Brook Avenue, Hattersley, where 17-year-old Edward Evans was found murdered, 26th October 1965.

Members of the public give information to help police in the Moors Murders body search, 26th October 1965.

Detective Chief Superintendent Arthur Benfield and Chief Superintendent K Frost on Saddleworth Moor looking for the bodies killed by Ian Brady and Myra Hindley, 27th October 1965.

Police search Saddleworth Moor for the bodies of the missing children who were murdered by Ian Brady and Myra Hindley, 28th October 1965.

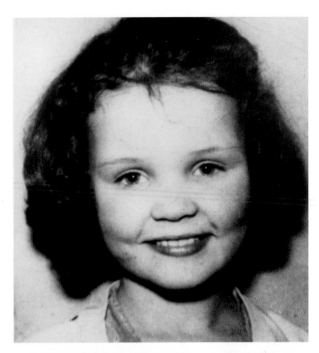

Lesley Ann Downey, aged 10, victim of the Moors Murderers, Ian Brady and Myra Hindley, December 1965.

12-year-old Patricia Hodges, a witness in the Moors Murders case, December 1965.

Detective Policewoman Margaret Campion, involved in the Moors Murders case, 13th December 1965.

Maureen Smith, the sister of Moors Murderer Myra Hindley, with her husband
David Smith during the hearing at Hyde, Greater Manchester, 9th December 1965.

Patricia Ann Hodges, the schoolgirl who was befriended by Moors Murderers Myra Hindley and Ian Brady, and who later gave evidence in their murder trial, 4th May 1966.

Ian Brady's house in Wardle Brook Avenue, Hattersley, where 17-year-old Edward Evans was found murdered, 26th October 1965.

Evans, Brady admitted to having murdered people in the past, and though momentarily fearful for his life, he overlooked the admittance as bragging to remain superior in David's eyes or a direct result of the drinks they had over the course of the evening.

In his later years, David would admit that he was a rebel in those days, idolising a Greaser culture that created images like James Dean, and sporting a teenage bad attitude that invited trouble. It was likely that Brady felt he could groom the boy, create an additional partner to their crimes. Often the two men would stay up drinking and handling the guns on the table. In his younger years, David did not recognise the testing of the older man as he told him plans for robberies or killing people, mostly in relation to the guns. Even on drunken nights when Brady bragged about previous murders and suggested that later, he would invite David to participate in the events. Much of these types of conversations occurred after their women had gone to bed, later in the night.

The Worst Night Ever

The night that would change David's life forever began when Myra Hindley appeared at the door of the flat that he and Maureen shared with Myra and Maureen's mother. She told David that she needed someone to escort her home, as it was dark, and she was afraid to walk alone. She even told David that Brady had some miniature wine bottles for him and they were waiting for him to pick them up. Once at 16 Wardle Brook Avenue, Manchester, she asked him to wait a moment for a signal before entering. Confused, he did as she asked. The lights flickered, and Brady answered the door, loudly asking if David wanted the miniature bottles of wine. Myra brought him to the kitchen and Brady returned to the other room, Myra handed him the bottles and went off after Brady into the other room. Barely moments later, a shockingly loud scream filled the building and Myra yelled for David to hurry into the sitting room and help them.

He rushed into the room; there he was shocked and frozen by what he saw. It did not seem to be real and his mind, unable to place the occurrences and make sense of what he saw, recognised the body as a life-size rag doll. Brady dropped it onto the floor, mere feet from David who could not say a word as his mind tried to wrap itself around what was happening. In the back of his mind, he recognised these events, and rising to the surfaces was a deathlike fear that chilled him throughout this body. The doll groaned, Brady raised his axe and smashed it into the head of the doll, but his mind was recognising the doll as what it was, a young man. A boy, no older than himself, and still David did not move and he could not speak. Somehow, he managed not to run from the room screaming murder, and if he had he very likely would have joined the boy on the floor. When the boy made a sound as if a groan again, Brady again brought the axe down onto his head, smashing it in deeply. The only sound the boy made after the second axing was a gurgling sound. Brady placed a bag over his head, wrapped an electrical cord around the boy's neck, and while strangling the boy shouted "You fucking dirty bastard" like a mantra.

In later years, he recalled that he was terrified and used every ounce of willpower to remain calm enough to keep himself alive by assisting them in moving the body and cleaning up. They wrapped the body in plastic and moved it to the spare bedroom. All along talking of how the body would be moved to the Moors on the very next day, and that David could help. Even as an adult he could not fathom how he had managed to stand there so calmly, to help with the blood and moving the body. He still remembers the blood, the pieces of skin and hair. Yet in the back of his mind, he kept reminding himself that one wrong move would add a second body to their list and he would never return home again. He had to remain calm, compliant, careful to seem as if he was purely interested and not waiting carefully for his chance to escape the insanity that he had just witnessed. The readings that Brady had shared with him came to mind in those moments, a pure understanding that Brady would not doubt that killing David too was an acceptable action if it meant keeping his secrets.

The couple joked with each other about previous murders and drank a cup of tea. During the entire event, David could not stop wondering if he would leave or die that night. To increase his chances of surviving the night, David helped with everything they requested and tried to keep his wits about him, but he also hurried to get through it. While they were moving the body, Brady bragged that the others were in the Moors and that David must come back the next day and help move the body there with them. David was sick, scared, and when they were finished he nearly ran the entire way back to the flat that he shared with Maureen. He was still careful though, walking the first few blocks until he was sure he was out of sight of the psychopaths. Waking Maureen up, he was covered in blood and sick to his stomach. He quickly told her the things that he had seen, what Brady and her sister had done, and Maureen knew he could not be lying. It was not only the way in which he was visibly shaken that gave credence to his story, but also in the fact, that Maureen and her mother had recognised concerning changes in Myra ever since she had begun a relationship with Brady. They agreed they would go to the police in the morning.

Trials and Accusations

David was 17 and Maureen was 19 when they walked down the chilled street, scared for their own lives, and carrying a screwdriver and kitchen knife with them as they hurried to the nearby phone box to call the police and tell them the night's events. They were very afraid while they waited for the police and hid in the bushes to prevent anyone noticing them. At the Hyde Police Station, they told their story to the local police and then again to Superintendent Talbot. Amazed at the tale, the police took two dozen officers to the site of the crime, and easily located the body and the axe in the room where David had reported it. Myra had not wanted to provide the police with the key to the room, claiming at first not to have it, but she had finally given in, and Brady was immediately arrested. At the station, Brady claimed that there had been a fight between Edward, David, and himself. Brady continued with his lies by claiming that he and David had killed the boy and that Hindley had not taken part in any of it.

In 1966, David would be instrumental in his testimony required to convict Brady and Hindley for the murders and he would later try to assist in finding the other bodies in the Moors. However, to discredit him and involve him in their punishment, both Brady and Hindley tried to implicate David in their crimes. The police even forced him to look at the photographs of Lesley Ann Downey and listen to the tape, as they believed him a suspect in the murder and demanded he make a full confession. They accused him of being the actual murderer in some of the killings and at least a willing participant in the others. Adding to this was the revelation of his own teenage delinquencies and the fact that he had accepted payment as part of his testimony to a newspaper. These events resulted in him having severe difficulty in finding work, Maureen and David's children were spat at in the streets, and the suspicion that he had actually been involved resulted in numerous fights in the local streets and pubs. Even detectives were part of the punishment, as they worked endlessly to try to get him to admit his personal guilt and reveal the locations of additional bodies of missing children.

The events of that awful last night with Brady and Hindley would haunt him, causing nightmares when he slept. It was as if he would be cursed to relive that moment of Edward's last breath over and over again, with no one to talk to and the pressures from locals and accusers who believed Hindley and Brady, his life would become a complete catastrophe. During the few years to follow, his situation would continue to get worse until his children were no longer living at home. He was jailed for attacking someone with a knife after a beating he received in a local pub, and then his wife, Maureen abandoned him and their three boys for another man. The stress of everything overwhelmed her and resulted in her complete abandonment of everything. Neither coped well with the results of their honesty and attempt to help others. David had been suicidal up until he met Mary, his second wife, in 1971 after his release from prison. That time spent in prison would be the very last time that David would have any negative interactions with the law, though he would still try to be helpful in regards to solving the mystery of Keith Bennett.

David tried on numerous occasions to help the police by giving them information of places that Hindley and Brady had taken the young couple, but had mostly been ignored after they had determined he was not a suspect. Some senior officers, particularly Detective Chief Inspector Joe Mounsey, did not believe that Smith was involved in the murders and some even felt that he should have received a medal. However, not many people agreed and he was never honoured for his courage. Later, he would also work with the Bennett family, to try to locate the last missing child of the Moors Murders. It was one of his wishes to help to return the boy to his family before his death, having many years being given the responsibility as part of the blame; he took to heart his responsibility to be part of the solution. Regardless of the challenges he met after going to the police about the Brady and Hindley murders, he never regretted having turned lives, and he himself could not have lived with the memory of not reported them. Mary strongly supported him, and her strength helped him cope with the innuendos of the media and others during the early years.

Nearly a New Beginning

Over the years, David credited Mary for the amazing changes in his life. He was completely in love with her and viewed her as his strength and his greatest supporter. Together they gained custody of his sons and had a daughter together. They too would be tormented by endless verbal and physical abuse, such as rocks being thrown through their front window, but together they endured. The most difficult challenges were how the children were treated, and that his children's pet rabbits were killed as well. The support of Mary's family was helpful to the couple, and their support of each other enabled them to survive the challenges. Together Mary and David raised their four children with little involvement from the Hindley family and they attempted to protect them from the media and the conspiracy that Myra worked to instigate. During the years, Maureen was rarely involved with the boys. She died from a brain tumour in 1980. For many years, due to Myra Hindley's claims of innocence, David and his family would experience increased media coverage and cruelty from people who did not believe his innocence. Mary and David struggled to keep jobs and in the 1990s, they moved to Ireland, finally to peace.

to peace.

A few other challenges would occur in Oughterard, specifically after Myra Hindley's death and some said their family was forced out of the area, but it was the abuse that made it so difficult to stay. Mary and David met their challenges after the 90s with much more patience and stamina than David had ever mustered in the earlier years, some believed it was due to age, and others believed it was thanks to the strength of Mary and her unending determination to remind him that he was a hero for what he had done. Much of the violence and threats were reduced in Ireland, which was a blessing to the family.

While in Ireland, Mary and David felt at home and David was a regular visitor to a local pub called the Back Room in Oughterard, which was not far from their home in Connemara. Many people knew David and talked about him as a gentle and friendly person who enjoyed a good drink and was great in conversation. Their life was much improved from their experiences in England and though recognised as English, they were welcomed, and people did not judge him or treat the family poorly. They finally had a place to call home where they did not have to spend all of their time worrying about the next time that the Moors Murderers would make headlines and awaken all the history again. His family was no longer tormented and he could live his life in a cottage that he and his wife refurbishing themselves. Over the years, David's family would grow and remain close, his children brought him grandchildren, and he even lived to see his great granddaughter.

The Death of David

David died at age 65 due to cancer. Mary and David were married for 40 years, and they ran a guesthouse in Galway. Mary said her only wishes are for everyone to remember David as she remembers him, the hero who ended the Moors Murderers' killing spree. During his last days, he lived with his wife in Connemara, and often shared company with his family, even great grandchildren. At the time of his death, he did not want his wife to experience the pain of watching someone take their very last breath of air, and he sent her from the room on an invented errand. When she returned, he had died David left behind a book he co-wrote named *Evil Relations*, which is the story of the challenges and torment he suffered over the years following his reporting of the murder to the police. It shares his experiences and his personal feelings that guided him during those dark days that began with the witnessing of a murder. The book was nominated for the Crime Writers' Association Gold Dagger Award for non-fiction, and David was proud of this accomplishment. His life will always be wrought with controversy about his involvement, but many people will remember him as a hero who put an end to the Moors Murders and as a survivor of the atrocities that Brady and Hindley inflicted on the world, their crimes to include purposefully causing him continued pain long into his adulthood.

He rushed into the room; there he was shocked and frozen by what he saw. It did not seem to be real and his mind, unable to place the occurrences and make sense of what he saw, recognized the body as a life-size rag doll. Brady dropped it onto the floor, mere feet from David who could not say a word as his mind tried to wrap itself around what was happening. In the back of his mind, he recognized these events, and rising to the surfaces was a deathlike fear that chilled him throughout this body. The doll groaned, Brady raised his axe and smashed it into the head of the doll, but his mind was recognizing the doll as what it was, a young man. A boy, no older than himself, and still David did not move and he could not speak. Somehow, he managed not to run from the room screaming murder, and if he had he very likely would have joined the boy on the floor. When the boy made a sound as if a groan again, Brady again brought the axe down onto his head, smashing it in deeply. The only sound the boy made after the second axing was a gurgling sound. Brady placed a bag over his head, wrapped an electrical cord around the boy's neck, and while strangling the boy shouted "You fucking dirty bastard" like a mantra.

Chapter 7

Arrest
and Trials

Arrest and Trials

Ian's suitcases were filled with what David had described as 'dodgy stuff'. There were a lot of pornographic magazines and weapons, including a cosh, a knife and a gun. There were erotic books, diaries, and Nazi paraphernalia. Most interesting was a reel-to-reel tape. When they played it, they heard the voice of a little girl crying for her mother, as well as the voices of two adults, including a woman who spoke harshly to the child and advised her to do what she was told. There were also images of a little girl wearing nothing but shoes and socks, lying down, praying and standing with her arms outstretched.

Following David Smith's revelations about Myra and Ian, the police were cynical that anything about the story was true. David didn't seem to be quite all there, they thought, and they were far from convinced that he was telling the truth. It's not unknown for the mentally unstable to fabricate unlikely tales. Still, they had no choice but to investigate everything.

The three policemen, Fairley, Carr, and Talbot, got into a car and drove up to Hattersley, where Myra was living, still with her Gran, in their nice new council house. Ian wasn't an official resident, but he was there so much of the time he might as well have been. Gran had grown used to having him around. They didn't interact much, but he wasn't much bother and he seemed to make Myra happy.

Myra and Gran's very ordinary house was, David had told the coppers, where he had witnessed this Eddie being killed and where he had felt compelled, for reasons of his own safety, to assist with the cleanup of the body. If the story he told was true, there should be ample evidence of a crime.

As the policemen drove into the estate, it occurred to Talbot that maybe a disguise would be in order, so he pulled over a delivery van that was bringing bread from house to house, and asked the driver if he could borrow his basket and coat. Bemused, and unaware that he was about to participate in the arrest of the century, the driver obliged.

Bob Talbot, now dressed up as a bread delivery-man, knocked on Myra's door and she answered. She was already prepared for work with her characteristic hair-do and heavy make-up. She was none too happy about being disturbed when she was about to go out, especially as she hadn't ordered any bread to be delivered – and, one presumes, because she was a little perturbed by the knowledge of the body upstairs, waiting to be disposed of later. She looked at Bob and asked him rather impatiently what he wanted. She had to go to work. She didn't have time to be messed around.

The policeman identified himself and demanded to see Ian, saying that he knew he was in the house. Myra protested that there was no man in the house at all, but Talbot made his way in the back door, while Fairley and Carr let themselves in the front.

Ian was not as organised as Myra. He was still in his underwear on the sofa bed in the front room. He looked up as the policemen came in, and in that instant understood exactly what was going on; he'd been busted. Despite his conviction that his crimes were "perfect" and would never be discovered, he'd made one of the most basic mistakes of all, and had shared his secret world with someone who wasn't ready for the challenge. David wasn't the man he thought.

But he wasn't going to give in that easily. Ian had talked himself out of a sticky situation more than once before; maybe he'd manage to do it again.

Myra and Ian had often talked about what they would do if they were ever apprehended. They had retreated so far into a fantasy world that they imagined they'd be able to grab some of their weapons and blast their way out, just like the cowboys they saw in the films they watched at the cinema. The police would just fall away as they waved their guns about, and let bullets fly through the air. They had imagined themselves leaping onto a motorcycle or into a getaway car and making a daring escape, the sort of escape performed only by the best.

Or at least that's what Myra seemed to believe. It is possible than Ian was a little more pragmatic; he wrote later that he had always intended to kill himself and Myra if it came to it; that'd he'd rather die by his own hand than be taken in by any copper. He'd kill the arresting officer first, then Myra and then himself. In that way, they'd go down in a blaze of glory and he would be remembered as the special man that he was, and not as some sort of a pathetic wretch, cking out his days in prison like so many of the men and boys whom he'd known growing up.

But despite the fact that they had murdered someone right there in the house the night before, the guns were upstairs, and there was no way that either Ian or Myra could reach them. There was going to be no daring escape, no blaze of glory, or romantic murder/suicide. All that remained was a grubby little crime – and the inconvenient fact of the body upstairs. Their best hope was to convince the police that nothing untoward had gone on around there, and that there was nothing to be seen. Failing that, they would have to fall back on a plan b.

Very calmly, Talbot informed the pair that he had been informed that an 'act of violence' had occurred in the house the previous night, and that he had come to investigate it. Myra offered no resistance to his request to search the house; possibly she thought that if she appeared to be calm and cooperative, it would all go away.

The officers trudged upstairs where they found Gran, understandably frightened by all the hullaballoo, perched on the edge of her bed. Gran had heard someone screaming the night before, but Myra had told her that it was just her, and that she'd hurt herself in a minor accident. Gran had no idea that someone had been killed downstairs while she had been lying in bed. Now she was astonished to see the police traipsing about her house. She had no idea what was going on. Myra assured her that everything would be OK and told her that she'd bring her a cup of tea. Myra had always been fond of

Gran, and she was not going to let her be unduly upset or disturbed by the heavy-booted policemen stamping around. Perhaps she also thought that the touching sight of a young woman being so solicitous of her grandmother would make them think that there was nothing to see, and go away.

Talbot peered into all the rooms in the small house, bar one, which was locked. Myra explained that this was where she kept her guns and that she kept it locked for safety. She explained that she was the member of a local gun club, and of course, extremely careful with her weapons. You wouldn't want to leave a room with guns in it unlocked. A child might walk in off the street and do itself an injury. No, she was a responsible gun owner and she would never let such a thing happen.

Careful or not, at this, the officers' ears pricked up. One of the details in the unlikely story they had been told by David the evening before, was that there were several guns in the house. If one element of the story was true, that lent some credence to the rest! They demanded that Myra open the door of the room so that they could see for themselves what was inside.

'The key's at work,' Myra explained. She went on to say that it would not be convenient for her to go to work and retrieve it, and acquired a petulant tone and expression. The policemen, however, were not going to take no for an answer, and started preparing to kick down the door.

At this point, Ian took charge. He told Myra to give the officers the key to the room, which she had had in her handbag all along.

Inside the room there was a bed, and some basic bedroom furniture. And on the bed there was a large bundle wrapped in a dark blanket. A human foot was clearly visible at one end of it. Here was the dead body of which David Smith had spoken. It seemed, after all, that he had been telling the truth.

As Officer Talbot started to make arrangements for the body to be examined, Ian began to offer an explanation for the body that was so inconveniently in Myra's house. He said that there had been an argument, and that things had 'got out of hand.' They had been drinking, and one thing had led to another. There had never been any intention that someone would get hurt.

Ian was cautioned, but Myra, who appeared to be simply the aggressor's girlfriend, was not. Nonetheless, she insisted on coming along to the station to support Ian, and she picked up her little dog, Puppet, to bring along.

Ian was cuffed, and faced the humiliation of being paraded out to the car in front of a gaggle of curious neighbours. Another police car had arrived, with David sitting sombrely in the back seat. Myra fixed David with a steely gaze, but Ian just smirked.

First experience with the law

At the station, Ian was taken away for questioning. Despite everything that had happened, Myra was calm. She waited while a policewoman was fetched to interview her, drinking tea and petting Puppet as though she had not witnessed a man being killed just the night before.

The story Ian told was both sordid and simple. He insisted that there had been no intention of hurting anyone. He and Eddie had met in the city the evening before, and had spent their time together drinking heavily. They had got into a stupid, drunken argument and ended up falling to blows. He suggested that Eddie was gay, and that the intention had been to blackmail him. Ian insisted that David Smith, not him, had been the one to make things escalate, when he started to hit Eddie with a stick. In this state of panic, Ian said, he had hit Eddie with an axe, and he had died shortly after that. Still drunk and by now confused and panic-stricken, Ian and David had cleaned up the scene, and carried Eddie's body upstairs so that they could dispose of it later when things calmed down.

So far, it looked as though Ian's story was likely to be accurate. It wouldn't be the first time two drunken idiots had started taking pops at each other, only for it all to end much more badly than necessary. By the time Detective Chief Superintendent Benfield was on the scene, it looked as though everything would be wrapped up in a matter of days.

Talbot and Benfield returned to Myra's house where they

photographed the body and everything with it, including a number of books that Ian had been reading. Eddie's trousers were open, they noted, and there was a letter in his pocket from a girl called Wendy.

The officers extended their search to the rest of the house, collecting Ian's camera equipment, photographs and negatives, as well as blood stained clothing and samples of hair.

Meanwhile, Myra was finally being interviewed by a woman police officer, Margaret Campion, who was finding her rather difficult. She insisted that she was telling the same story as Ian – that it had been a normal evening that had all gone horribly wrong. However, there was one telling detail that suggested that all might not be as it initially appeared; whereas Ian had told the police that they had spent the whole evening in Manchester, Myra said that they had been walking on the moors before meeting Eddie. In any case, she insisted that Eddie's death had been nothing but an unfortunate accident. Things had simply got out of hand. Myra also insisted that David, not Ian, had been the chief aggressor, and was really the person responsible for Eddie's demise. Crossly, she repeated that the police should be talking to David, not to her. She didn't understand why David hadn't been arrested and why they were giving her so much hassle.

While the forensic evidence was being gone through, the unfortunate Eddie's mother came to identify the battered and almost unrecognisable body of her son. He had been seventeen years old, barely a man. He had only just started to live.

At half past six that evening, a fateful discovery was made. Benfield returned to Myra's house to see if there was anything else the police should investigate. It was getting dark and the curious neighbours had receded for the evening. Almost on a whim, Benfield decided to see if Myra's car would yield any information. There was a wallet on the dashboard, which he picked up and looked inside, where he found three sheets of paper. No doubt expecting to see a shopping list, or perhaps some documents relating to work, what he found instead was a detailed list relating to how to clean up after a murder and establish an alibi. The list had been written with many abbreviations, but it was still perfectly clear what it was for. Eddie's death had just become a great deal more interesting. Benfield's suspicion was that the plan had been written before he was killed – although Ian protested to the contrary – and that made it cold-blooded, premeditated murder. A reference in the note to Penistone, a town some distance away in the Pennines, suggested that Ian had intended to get rid of the body there, but for some reason had not – perhaps because of the sprained ankle that Ian had suffered during the attack, or maybe because he felt sufficiently confident that David would not go to the authorities, and he'd wait until he had time to dispose of the body in his own time.

In fact, despite having gone to the police with his story, David was still a suspect. The whole thing seemed very odd, and he had freely admitted to helping to clean up the scene of the killing. Could it be that he had been a willing participant who had subsequently developed a case of cold feet? However, there was nothing to pin on him, and he was allowed to go home. Before he left, the policemen asked him if he had any ideas about how to get Myra and Ian to squawk. David offered that Ian was afraid of spiders, and would get very upset if one was put into his cell, and that Myra loved her dog so much that if Puppet was threatened to be hurt, or killed, she'd tell them whatever they wanted to know. While David was being helpful, he didn't seem to quite believe what was going on himself. Could he be trusted about anything?

The First Charge of Murder

Ian was charged with murder that evening. He continued to insist that his account of the evening was perfectly accurate. As there was no sufficient evidence to charge her with a crime, Myra was allowed to leave, but not to return home; her house was still a crime scene, and the police were far from finished with it. Instead, she went back to her mother's house where she told Nellie everything – or not everything, but what she felt it expedient for her to know. Nellie was upset, but took Myra's story at face value. After all, why would Myra want to kill a teenage boy? She had a good job and a normal life, and had no reason to do anything of the sort. And she was good to her Gran; she would never want to do anything to hurt the old lady.

It had not yet occurred to anyone that what they were dealing with, was much more than just the death of one poor unfortunate.

By this stage, Eddie's death had made the newspapers and Myra's old friends and neighbours were all agog with the revelation that she and her boyfriend had been involved in the teenager's demise. Former classmates remembered times when Myra had been rough with them. But still, nobody believed that she herself could have done that much. It must have been Ian. They'd always known that he was a bad sort.

Tom Craig, Myra's boss, came to Nellie's house to inform Myra that while he would keep her job open for her until it was all resolved, Ian would not be welcome back, even if he was cleared. The best case scenario was that Ian had been up to no good with the dead teenager – even if it turned out not to be cold-blooded murder, he was not the sort of person whom anybody would want to have on the staff. The fact that it does not seem to have occurred to Tom to consider that Myra might have been culpable, says legions about the trust he had in his young employee. Many bosses would have not hesitated to lay a worker off in such a circumstance – and in fact Myra would have preferred it, as then she'd have been able to claim unemployment benefits – but Tom seems not to have wanted her to suffer just because she'd got mixed up with the wrong sort.

The Moors Enter the Investigation

A breakthrough occurred when Officer Ian Fairley was going through some notebooks that had been retrieved from Myra's house. Ian had done some rough sketches of gangsters, and had written a list of names. Most of the names referred to film stars of the day, but one was John Kilbride – a name that stood out immediately as belonging to the little boy who had gone missing in November 1963 from Ashton Market. What was little John's name doing in Ian's notebook?

Fairley's heart began to race as he realised that he might be onto something big. Together, the officers in charge of the case went through Ian's photographs. There were hundreds, and many of them that were perfectly ordinary, but a few stood out because they didn't seem to have any particular purpose – simple landscape shots that were mostly of the ground, rather than any particular view or panorama. They couldn't figure out exactly what the photographs were for, but a sort of instinct suggested that they were important. The missing children of Manchester were the object of huge local anxiety and an ongoing investigation. Could it possibly be that the answer to this riddle was right in front of them?

David Smith had told the police that Ian had boasted about hiding bodies on the moor, but nobody had taken this particularly seriously. Well, now they had more reason to think about it. Although there was one striking photograph of Myra's car against some distinctive black rocks, most of the photographs were so nondescript it was impossible to figure out where they had been taken. David Smith did his best to help, but he had not been able to identify the location either.

Although she didn't know it yet, Myra was experiencing her last few hours of freedom. She visited poor Gran, who was utterly befuddled by everything that was going on, and didn't know why Ian had been arrested. It was arranged that Gran would go and live with her daughter Annie. Myra asked a friend, Elsa, to take care of Puppet for the time being, and put together a 'care package' of food and books to bring to Ian at the station. When Ian saw Myra walking into the station between two policewomen, he assumed that she had been charged and arrested.

While Myra told Ian's lawyer that she agreed 100% with his version of events, and refused to cooperate with the police, a search was ongoing on the moors. The police were working with an officer who knew the area well, and were attempting to use Ian's photographs to identify spots of interest. Pressed to admit that the notes he had made referred to disposing of the bodies of the missing children, Ian insisted that they were to do with Eddie, and nobody else.

Myra is Implicated

Finally, Myra was informed that there was ample evidence to accuse her of being complicit in Eddie's death. The police no longer considered her to be 'just the girlfriend' of someone caught up in a teenager's sordid murder. Now she was being viewed as an accomplice. She was taken into a cell and told where to stand for her mug shot. In that instant, one of Britain's most iconographic images was taken. Myra would be haunted by it for the rest of her life.

Myra spent her first night in captivity in Risley Remand Centre near Warrington; Ian was already in the men's section. As rumours were already circulating among the prisoners that she and Ian were responsible for the deaths of the children who had disappeared, it was judged unsafe for her to be among the other prisoners. Neither Myra nor Ian dared to leave their cells, for fear of what would happen to them.

The Investigation Gathers Steam

While Ian and Myra prepared themselves for their trial, the police had made considerable progress. They had found a receipt from when Myra and Ian had hired a car – on the day of John Kilbride's disappearance – and they had identified some of the locations shown in Ian's photographs of the moors. A large number of policemen were investigating these areas in a very orderly manner, marching across the ground with sticks that they used to prod the ground to see if it had been interfered with. On the exposed moors, it was hard, tiring work, but if there was even the slightest chance that the children's bodies could be found, and their families given some relief after all their suffering, it would be worth it.

When the press got wind of the fact that the police were searching the moors, everything clicked into place. Not just the national, but the international press, swooped into Manchester to find out whatever they could about Myra, Ian, and the missing children. It was the perfect news story; plenty of photogenic victims, grieving families and a very odd young couple said to have been responsible for the crimes.

When she was questioned about John Kilbride's disappearance, Myra insisted that she had never been to Ashton Market, where he had last been seen, despite the fact that she had been there regularly, and that the police knew this, having been told so by her sister Maureen. The police switched tack and began to ask about little Lesley Ann Downey, who had last been seen in a fairground in Manchester. Again, Myra insisted that she knew nothing, and that she had never been to a fairground.

The search on the moors was intensifying. With the help of Myra's neighbour's daughter, Patty Ann Hodges, who had often accompanied Myra and Ian on jaunts to the moors, the police were able to narrow in on a specific area that could also be seen in Ian's photographs. Patty told Ian Fairley that she had been taken to the spot with Myra and Ian on several occasions, including one on Christmas Day the previous year, 24 hours before Lesley Ann's disappearance. But there were still no bodies.

In Manchester, David Smith was brought in once more for questioning. By now he was fed up. It was understandable, really. He had been getting a huge amount of attention from the police and the press – and all because he had tried to do the right thing. David admitted that he and Ian had often plotted to commit robberies. It was true that he had a history of petty crime – but didn't that make the fact that he'd gone to the police with what he knew about Eddie's murder all the more impressive? David's life had become a misery and he just wanted it all to be over.

A Breakthrough in the Case

David mentioned that Ian had had a lot of 'incriminating evidence' that he had kept in suitcases. David didn't know where the suitcases were, or exactly what the incriminating evidence was, but he did know that Ian had a fondness for railway stations.

This was the breakthrough the case needed. Officers all over Manchester went through left luggage at the stations, and the suitcases were located – and with them, the proverbial can of worms was opened.

Ian's suitcases were filled with what David had described as 'dodgy stuff'. There were a lot of pornographic magazines and weapons, including a cosh, a knife and a gun. There were erotic books, diaries, and Nazi paraphernalia. Most interesting was a reel-to-reel tape. When they played it, they heard the voice of a little girl crying for her mother, as well as the voices of two adults, including a woman who spoke harshly to the child and advised her to do what she was told. There were also images of a little girl wearing nothing but shoes and socks, lying down, praying and standing with her arms outstretched.

The little girl was Lesley Ann Downey, and the voices were, very clearly, those of Myra and Ian.

On the moors, there was another breakthrough when one of the officers noticed something that appeared to be a white, withered stick, emerging from the peat. They dug, and found Lesley Ann's naked, partially preserved body. What remained of her arm had been extruding from the peat, almost as though it were beckoning to them, and saying, 'Here I am. Take me home.' The half of the body that had been in the peat was intact; half of her face was still there, and still recognisable as belonging to the pretty little girl who was so desperately missed by her family.

Although a considerable amount of time had passed, it was evident from the postmortem that little Lesley Ann had probably been smothered.

Myra and Ian appeared in court to be formally charged with one of the last of their murders, and the first to be discovered. Later the same day they were confronted with the discovery of the tapes and Lesley Ann's body. When the tape of Lesley Ann's desperate pleas was played, Myra started to sob, but she refused to speak.

By now, the police were sure that Ian and Myra were behind the disappearance of the rest of the missing children – John Kilbride, Keith Bennett, Pauline Reade, and a girl called Susan Omrod, who had vanished just three and a half months before. However, there was nothing that they could use to formally link them. They continued to search the desolate moors, doing their best to match the often almost featureless landscape with Ian's black-and-white photographs. Morbid sightseers had taken to setting up shop whenever a search was ongoing, driving up from the city in their cars and enjoying flasks of tea and picnics, as they watched the men at work.

Another Piece of the Puzzle
Falls Into Place

Then, during yet another search of Myra's house, one of the officers found another piece of crucial evidence. Tucked inside the spine of a prayer book that Myra had received as a gift on the occasion of her First Holy Communion, there was a receipt for two more suitcases, deposited this time at Manchester Central Station.

Meanwhile, just when it was beginning to seem as though the endless searches of the moor were pointless, the police managed to match the skyline captured in one of Ian's photographs with a particular spot. Digging, they quickly found the putrefied remains of young John Kilbride. Despite the body's state of decomposition, it was evident that John had been subjected to sexual abuse, probably rape, before he was killed.

Many of the police officers were family men with children of their own. One can only imagine how difficult it must have been for them to have to deal with the tragic, gruesome remains of Myra and Ian's victims before returning home.

John Kilbride's family had long since given up any hope that their little boy was safe. In a way, it was a relief that he was found and that at last they could have a funeral and lay him to rest. Lesley Ann's family felt much the same way.

There was still a lot of police work to be done in terms of definitively proving that Myra and Ian were the ones responsible for Lesley Ann and John's awful deaths. Painstaking work was able to match marks on the wall captured in the photos of Lesley Ann's naked body, with those in Myra's house.

Aware that they could never cover every square inch of the moors on their own, the police started to distribute copies of Ian's photographs to cyclers and hikers in the Manchester area, in the hope that they might be able to help. Hundreds of volunteers were on hand.

Appearing Before the Magistrates For the First Time

On 28 October, Myra and Ian appeared before magistrates for the first time, and the wheels of justice were put into motion. Ian wore a simple grey suit, but Myra appeared to have dressed up for the occasion, in a bright red coat and with her striking bleached hair freshly set. The public gallery went wild with anger when they walked in. Among them were family members of little Lesley Ann.

Despite the mounting evidence against them, Ian and Myra refused to cooperate. They were confronted with photographs of themselves posing on their victim's graves, but would not acknowledge that they had done anything wrong. When it was suggested to Myra that the photographs had been taken when they had gone to ensure that the graves had not been disturbed, and so that they would remember the location, she refused to accept this, and continued to attempt to implicate David Smith.

Because Myra was so hard to crack, back in the station, the police officers decided that they would try to shock her into making an admission of guilt. They put together a book of Ian's landscape photographs, juxtaposed with grisly postmortem images of the children's bodies. Myra was shocked; she pushed the book away and shouted that she did not want to look at the photographs.

Ian was more forthcoming. He admitted that he had discussed burying bodies on the moor with David Smith, that he had taken pornographic images of little Lesley Ann and knew where she was buried, and that he had deliberately taken photographs of Myra smiling over John Kilbride's grave. However, he insisted that he was not responsible for any deaths other than that of Eddie, and that Eddie's death had been an accident, and certainly not cold-blooded murder. Despite all the evidence against them, both Ian and Myra insisted on their innocence when they were charged with Lesley Ann's murder.

As part of the police investigation, Myra's dog Puppet – which had been sent to stay at the local RSPCA kennels – was brought to a vet to have its age confirmed. An anaesthetic was administered so the dog could be x-rayed. Puppet reacted badly to the anaesthesia, and died. On hearing the news, Myra went berserk, screaming and accusing the police of being murderers, with no apparent understanding of the bitter irony in her words. Many people had observed over the years that Myra appeared to be fonder of dogs than of people, but they had had no idea just how accurate this observation really was.

The Remand Hearing

Myra and Ian's remand hearing was initiated on 4 November 1965, amid huge press and public interest. The newspapers spoke of little else, and Myra and Ian's names were on the lips of practically every person in Manchester. All the children who had been warned by their mum and dad to be careful, because kids were going missing in Manchester, could finally play in the streets without worrying that some nameless stranger would spirit them away. Myra's old friends and acquaintances racked over their memories of her as a young girl, trying to see in them some premonition of the monster she had apparently become. In most respects she had been a perfectly ordinary girl and adolescent, who had played games with the other children, and muddled through school and life as best she could.

On November 10, despite the fact that not all the missing children had been found, the search of the moors was called off. Quite simply, the area was far too vast to keep searching; it was the proverbial needle in a haystack.

The remand hearing seemed to have had an air of unreality for Myra, who appeared to have believed that her protests might somehow get her let off. Ian, however, was under no such illusion.

On the day when the prosecution laid out the evidence against the pair, he told Myra that to him, prison was a 'living death' and 'something he couldn't endure.' Ian's mother had brought him a bottle of jam, and he told Myra that he intended to break it and use the glass to kill himself, telling her that she would never be found guilty if she went on trial without him.

One of the hearing's most dramatic moments occurred when Lesley Ann Downey's mother took the stand. After giving her evidence, she was overcome with emotion, and started to scream at Myra: 'I'll kill you! I'll kill you'! She called her a tramp, and broke into sobs. Myra, who was usually expressionless, was upset by being called a tramp, and was comforted by Ian, who assured her that she was no such thing. Myra had always craved respect – she did not want to be discussed as though she were a common streetwalker! Her image had always been extremely important to her, as was respect from the people she interacted with. Why weren't they giving her the respect she deserved?

In the case against Ian and Myra with respect to the death of John Kilbride, the jacket in which his decayed body had been found was presented as evidence, still stinking of death.

During the remand hearings, it appears that Myra and Ian's predilection for erotica and violence remained unaffected. They spent their quiet time writing stories about children being sexually mistreated, encoding these so that they could enjoy them alone, and managed to pass notebooks and pieces of paper to each other surreptitiously when they were given the opportunity to meet. The couple also discussed their intention to get married, as they knew that if they were found guilty, they would only be allowed to see one another if they were man and wife. And, after all, they loved each other and had been made for one another. Marriage was simply the logical next step to take.

It must have been galling for the victims' families to know that, while Ian and Myra were at least being tried for the terrible things that they had done, they were not being mistreated. When Christmas came along, they were even allowed to celebrate, getting together on Christmas Eve for a special dinner with port wine and biscuits.

Myra wrote to her mother all about what she considered to be her ordeal, complaining that she was not being allowed to attend to her hair and that her dark roots were showing. It wasn't fair.

The Trial

After several months in prison, following the remand hearing and the ongoing inspection of evidence, Myra and Ian's trial was set for 19 April 1966. Over a hundred and fifty journalists descended on Chester, where the trial was to take place. Public feeling was running so high, that it was felt necessary to install special security screens to protect the accused. Attorney General Frederick Elwyn Jones represented the prosecution; Ian was defended by Emlyn Hooson, and Myra, by Godfrey Heilpern.

It was striking to note that Myra was very much the focus of the public's anger, despite the fact that Ian was accused of the same crimes, and was possibly even guiltier than she. The fact that she was a woman made her crimes seem even worse than they already were. How could a woman enjoy torturing and killing young children? It didn't seem to make any sense. People were fascinated by her appearance – the carefully bleached hair, her pale complexion, and strong, not unattractive features. Both Myra and Ian were compared to concentration camp guards – a comparison that they would doubtless have enjoyed. But true to form, Myra's appearance drew much more attention than Ian's. Women killers are rare, or at least less frequently apprehended, and are thereby considered fascinating creatures. Mythology abounds with stories of alluring women killers, and Myra was clearly a woman who spent a lot of time thinking about image and appearance. In particular, now that she was in prison and could not attend to the regular bleaching of her bouffant hair-do, her hair was changing colour. The Observer noted that it was different every week, 'first silver lilac, then bright canary blonde.' It also commented, rather snootily, on her style of dress, saying, 'At a glance, she looks as smartly turned out as a duchess, but when you look closer you see at once that this is mass-produced supermarket chic; there is an ambience of bubble gum and candyfloss.' The implication was that this was a working-class girl who had grown uppity, and acquired notions beyond her natural station in life. Somehow, this seemed to make her crimes even worse.

Despite the unflattering mug shot that is all most people know of Myra's appearance, reporters also commented on the fact that she was physically attractive, apparently aghast that a girl to whom one might a give second glance on the street, or even flirt with at a dance, could also be a cold-blooded killer. 'She is a big girl', one journalist wrote, 'with a striking face: fine straight nose, thinnish curved lips, rather hefty chin, and blue eyes. Full face she is almost a beauty.' Needless to say, no such detailed attention was given to Ian Brady's looks and sex appeal, or lack thereof.

Both David and Maureen Smith, who was heavily pregnant at the time, testified. They were brave to do so, as they had both been suffering in the outside world. Without access to the real killers, and refusing to believe that they had nothing to do with the case, the public had turned on them. David and Maureen had been dealing with hate mail and taunting, and even violent attacks. Nellie was no support to Maureen, having decided that Myra must be innocent and that she deserved her help. She had cut Maureen off and left her to fend for herself.

David was, of course, the chief witness for the prosecution. He had been present when Eddie was murdered, and who claimed to have heard Ian boasting that he had buried victims on the moor.

While David had been undeniably brave, heroic even, in going to the police, during the trial it emerged that he had signed a contract with a newspaper (which he initially refused to identify), and that he would receive £1000 (which was a lot of money at that time, especially for a young man with a small income and a baby on the way), for the right to syndicate his story should Ian and Myra be convicted for the crimes for which they were on trial. It emerged that the paper in question was the News of the World, and that it had already paid for David to have a holiday in France, and was giving him a weekly stipend as well as funding his stay in an expensive hotel for the duration of the trial. The News of the World, which had been founded in 1843, had built a business on printing the most scurrilous and scandalous stories it could find. In this case it had gone too far, and only narrowly escaped prosecution for having risked the integrity of the trial. This wouldn't be the last time the News of the World stepped into murky legal territory in its quest for the ultimate tell-all news story!

When Ian stepped into the dock, he stuck to the story that he had told the police; that Eddie had been killed in a drunken row (he admitted striking the fatal blow with an axe), and that David Smith had brought Lesley Ann to his house where he had taken pornographic images of her, but that she had left, unharmed, with David. He was not a good witness on his own behalf, making a number of slips that hinted at his guilt, such as when he mentioned covering Lesley Ann's face with a scarf 'just before the end', and referred to everybody getting dressed after the images of the naked child were taken, rather than just the little girl. Ian tried to help Myra get let off easily, insisting that she had only been there when he photographed Lesley Ann because he had made her, and that she had not been involved in any of his criminal activities.

Myra was deeply touched by Ian's solicitude. He must love her, if he was thinking only of her at such a difficult time! Both Ian and Myra believed that she would not receive a long sentence. They discussed how she would go on to live an adventurous life, and would write letters to Ian in jail, telling him all about it. Ian spoke for a total of eight hours.

When Myra finally took the dock, the first question she answered was about her feelings for Ian, asserting that she loved him. She went on to say that she was deeply ashamed of having participated in the pornographic shoot with Lesley Ann, and that she had only spoken to the child brusquely because she didn't want anyone to hear and find out what had been going on. Unconvincingly, she said that she had not been in the room when Ian removed Lesley Ann's clothing, and that she had been looking out the window when the pornographic photographs were shot, and had been running a bath when the little girl was finally killed after her ordeal. She insisted that she did not know anything about the landscape photographs; that she had had no idea that she was being shot anywhere near the graves of Ian's victims.

Finally, the prosecution and defence summed up. Predictably, the prosecution presented the pair as evil and unrepentant, with Myra involved in the murders every step of the way. Equally predictably, the defence suggested that there was little evidence to implicate Myra, and that she had been very much in the thrall of Ian, who had masterminded the whole thing. But no one who had looked into Myra's intelligent eyes could imagine her to be the passive girl in thrall to a stronger man who was using her like a puppet. This was a woman who knew her own mind and knew what she was doing.

While Myra knew by now that there was no hope for Ian, she still seemed to have believed that she could pin blame on David, and that, while she would be convicted of something, she would probably get off relatively lightly.

She was wrong.

Guilty!

After listening to the judge provide a summary of the evidence, which took a full five hours, the jury deliberated for two hours and fourteen minutes, emerging sombre-faced with their verdict: Ian was found guilty of all three of the murders for which the couple were being tried, and Myra for the murder of Eddie and Lesley Ann, and while not guilty of the murder of young John Kilbride, guilty of helping Ian to cover it all up. Both were sentenced to life in prison. Ian would be removed to Durham Prison, and Myra to Holloway Prison. The judge, Justice Atkinson, referred to Ian and Myra as 'two sadistic killers of the utmost depravity', and commented that while he felt that Ian was incapable of rehabilitation, there was hope for Myra when she was removed from her lover's influence.

Writing in The Guardian, journalist Geoffrey Whiteley described the scene:

Soon after 5 pm Brady and Hindley mounted the 18 steps into the glass-screened dock for the last time.

Suddenly the court clerk was reading the charges to the jury foreman. The answers came swiftly: Brady guilty of murdering Evans, Downey, and Kilbride; Hindley guilty of murdering Evans and Downey, not guilty of murdering Kilbride, but guilty of harbouring Brady.

Only Sentence

The Judge told Ian he would pass the only sentence the law now allowed. Ian, who seemed unmoved, walked down the dock steps flanked by two prison officers. Myra left the dock fully composed.

The Judge then turned to compliment the police. The murders, he said, had been brought to light by investigations of 'the utmost skill.' The finding of the left luggage ticket tucked down the spine of a Prayer Book belonging to Myra was the sort of thoroughness that had led to the case.

By extraordinary chance, the death penalty (which was by now very rarely appealed) had been abolished the very day on which Myra was arrested. Many felt that this was a case that should have ended in an execution, and that an exception should be made for anyone who killed a child. There seemed to be a lack of closure, to use a modern phrase. Everybody would have felt better if Ian and Myra had swung for their crimes, as they surely deserved to.

Nobody can know exactly what was going through the minds of Myra Hindley and Ian Brady as they were taken away to begin their long incarceration. Given that Ian had already sworn that he would commit suicide if forced to spend the rest of his life in jail, it is not difficult to imagine that he, too, might at this juncture have welcomed the prospect of an execution. One can only guess what went through the mind of Myra, who had remained so very impassive throughout her trial, and had never believed that she would be found guilty of the most dreadful of crimes.

Life Behind Bars

Myra was horrified by her treatment at Holloway Prison. She suffered the indignity of being searched for lice – in both the hair on her head, and in her pubic hair, and of being tested for venereal disease.

Prisoners who have been 'put away' for crimes against children always have a hard time in prison. They are referred to as 'nonces', and considered the lowest of the low. Everyone wants to hurt them, and the prison officers tend to turn a blind eye to their abuse. Myra was not just someone who had hurt and killed children, she was a *woman* who had done such awful things. To nobody's surprise, the other prisoners hated her, and she was badly attacked on a number of occasions.

Myra continued to hope that she would be set free and appealed over her conviction, saying that being tried with Ian had not helped her case. Nonetheless, she and Ian stayed in close contact, writing to each other frequently. He was having a hard time, too. He had been put into solitary confinement after the constant attacks, and was wiling away the days reading books from the prison library.

Myra had often felt rejected by her family, but they stood by her now, in her darkest hour. Nellie visited often, although she and Bob divorced, and he completely disowned his daughter. Gran knitted for Myra, and sent her warm clothing in jail. Even Maureen, who had been instrumental in getting Myra sent away, tried to stay in touch. She and David were still having a very hard time. Nobody wanted to work with him, they received a lot of hate mail, and a lot of people deflected their anger towards Myra and Ian onto the young couple.

Friends in High Places

Myra seemed to have acquired a certain amount of charisma. She was befriended by a number of prison visitors, some of whom were members of the aristocracy. Although she was not a lesbian by natural inclination, without access to the man she loved, Myra embarked on a number of lesbian affairs. With plenty of time on her hands, she read widely and studied for formal state qualifications, including taking an O-level in German.

Although Myra's life had acquired a degree of normality in the far-from-normal environment of the prison, and Myra and Ian were still under investigation. Little Keith Bennett and Pauline Reade were still missing, and the general assumption was that Myra and Ian were responsible. When Myra was questioned, however, she refused to provide any information, and continued trying to blame David for everything.

In the late 1960s, Myra was befriended by a man named Frank Pakenham, better known as Lord Longford. They would go on to have a long and much-discussed friendship. He was quickly convinced that Myra had been under Ian's spell, and could not be held responsible for the murders she had participated in. With his support, she renewed her interest in the Catholic faith. This newfound love of God seems to have been genuine, but Myra might also have been motivated by the thought that it could boost her chances of being accepted for parole. In 1970 she wrote to Lord Longford about her 'second chance,' saying:

'I wish I could put complete faith in God, but I'm frightened to do so, for my faith is full of doubt and despair that I'll never be good enough to merit complete forgiveness. I don't think I could adequately express just how much it means to me to have been to Confession and to have received Holy Communion. It is a terrifyingly beautiful thing – terrifying because I have taken a step which has taken me onto the threshold of a completely new way of life which demands much more from me than the previous one, and beautiful because I feel spiritually reborn. I made such a mess of my old life and I thank God for this second chance.'

When she reached her late twenties, Myra decided that she would finally cut her ties with Ian. She had convinced many of her friends and lovers that she was innocent of the crimes for which she had been convicted, or at least that her involvement had been simply because she was under Ian's spell. She embarked on a serious relationship with a woman she seems to have really loved, Tricia, who was a prison officer and a former nun. The pair fantasised about breaking Myra out of prison and starting out on a new life as missionaries in Brazil.

In the 1970s, Lord Longford's campaign to have Myra considered for release ramped up. The public was outraged, and nobody more so than the still grieving family of Lesley Ann. When it emerged that Myra had in fact been taken out of prison on a number of trips, to Hampstead Heath, and to an exhibition at the British Museum, there was uproar. Nobody – apart from Myra's friends and well-wishers – believed that she was capable of rehabilitation, or indeed that anyone should try rehabilitating her. Devastated by the growing realisation that she was unlikely to ever be free again, Myra retreated into the fantasy world in which she and Ian had spent so much of their time, and began dreaming and plotting an escape. The plot would never have worked, but when it was uncovered there was another trial, and Myra was given an additional twelve months to serve, on top of the life sentence she was already serving.

As the 1970s continued, Myra's supporters engaged in an active campaign to change public opinion towards her. and leaked her personal letters to the newspapers. Predictably, this move backfired, and people started to hate her all the more. Myra asked her supporters to stop campaigning for her, but the damage had already been done.

Although Myra had many friends among the other prisoners, the attacks didn't stop. Ten years after the trial that had put her away, she was violently attacked by another prisoner, and hurt so badly that she had to be sent to hospital (under a pseudonym) and treated. She was unable to eat solid food for more than a month.

In the 1980s, a new friend entered Myra's life: David Astor, the editor of The Observer newspaper, a very influential publication. Astor had worked in lobbying for many causes, such as the abolishment of apartheid, and Lord Longford asked him to consider taking on Myra's case. Like Lord Longford, David Astor was quickly convinced that Myra had been under Ian's influence and that she was capable of rehabilitation, and maybe, one day, release.

A Model Student

In 1977, Myra was transferred to Durham Prison, where the conditions were much harsher than they had been in Holloway. She was very unhappy; things hadn't been easy before, and she had been subjected to a number of attacks, but she had managed to build a sort of life for herself behind bars. Now she felt as though she was back to square one. At least she was able to continue with her studies, on which she had already embarked.

In 1980, her sister Maureen, who was just thirty-four, died tragically of a brain haemorrhage. Not long afterwards, Myra's father Bob died. Like Maureen, ever since Myra's arrest, Bob had been suffering for what she had done. He, too, had been physically attacked and tormented in his home. No doubt the constant stress of these experiences had contributed to both deaths.

In 1983, Myra was relieved to be transferred from the grimness of Durham Prison, to Cookham Wood, in Kent. It was a much more pleasant atmosphere. She had lots of time to study, and was allowed to decorate her cell as she wanted.

Myra had cut off her ties with Ian, but in the public's mind they would forever be associated. He was having a far more bleak time than Myra. She had visitors and was still loved by what remained of her family, but nobody ever visited him.

In 1985, the Parole Board announced that Myra would have to serve at least another five years. She was devastated. Her hopes had been raised - only to be dashed again.

Justice for Keith Bennett and Pauline Reade?

Then things got even worse. Myra had always denied having had anything to do with the deaths of little Keith Bennett and the pretty teenager Pauline Reade, but in 1985, Ian discussed their murders, implicating Myra. Keith's mother Winnie wrote to Myra, begging her to reveal whatever she knew about Keith's death, and the whereabouts of his body, but Myra insisted that she knew absolutely nothing. Winnie asked Myra if they could meet, but Myra was advised against it.

Following Ian's revelations, the search of the moors was renewed. Peter Topping, the man in charge of the search, came to Myra and asked her to help by looking at maps and photographs of the moors. She agreed, but never gave the slightest admission of guilt, saying instead that she would see if she could identify any areas that had been of interest to Ian. The Home Secretary of the time, Douglas Hurd, gave Topping permission to take Myra to the moor if that was necessary. Of course, such a visit would have to be surrounded in secrecy. If the media found out about it they would have a field day, and then there was the issue of Myra's own safety.

On 16 December 1986, Myra was woken early in the morning and brought to Maidstone, where a helicopter was waiting for her. She was brought back to the moors in Manchester, where she had spent so many happy hours in the heyday of her love relationship with Ian. There, she was dressed like the rest of the search party. She identified a number of places of potential interest, but refused to admit that she knew anything about where any of the victims had been killed, sticking to her story that she had not been directly involved in any murder.

When the media found out that Myra had been let out of jail for the purpose of searching for the bodies, both the journalists and the public expressed their absolute horror.

Myra must have known that nobody believed that she was innocent of Keith and Pauline's deaths, and in February 1987, she finally came clean about what everybody already knew and made a full confession. She continued, however, to deny any involvement in the other murders, and insisted that she had only been involved because she was so besotted with Ian, who had absolute power over her. Shortly afterwards she wrote an 'open letter' to Ian via the BBC, urging him to cooperate with the police, as she had done.

With Myra's help, the body of Pauline Reade was finally discovered in July 1987. The peat ground of the moor had preserved her body very well. It was easy to see that she had been killed by an injury to her throat, and that she had suffered a sexual assault. For Pauline's family, it was good news that she could finally be returned to them for burial. For Keith's mother Winnie, it was a knife in an ever-raw wound. Where was Keith? She was getting older. Would his body be recovered while she was still alive, so that she would at least have the peace of mind of knowing that he had finally received the dignified funeral that he deserved?

A few days later, Ian was also taken from prison to visit the moor, in the hope that he would indicate where Keith's body lay. He provided no help whatsoever, but seemed to enjoy the day out and the views across the moor.

A photograph of Moors Murderer, Ian Brady, 7th May 1966.

Moors Murderers Ian Brady and Myra Hindley, a clerk and a shorthand-typist are seen leaving court in a police van after the couple have been sentenced, 7th May 1966.

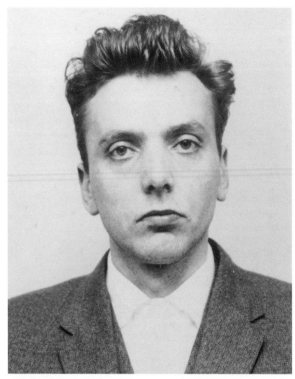

Ian Brady is sentenced to life imprisonment for murder, 7th May 1966.

David Smith, brother-in-law of Myra Hindley, 1966.

The scene of Edward Evans' murder at the residence of Ian Brady, 16 Wardle Brook Avenue, 1966.

A photograph of Central Station, where Ian Brady and Myra Hindley left evidence connected to their murders, 1966.

A police photograph of Myra Hindley upon her arrest, 1966.

Millward Merchandise, the workplace where Ian Brady and Myra Hindley met, 1966.

Chief Arthur Benfield addresses his staff in the hunt for the bodies of the children who were killed by Ian Brady and Myra Hindley on Saddleworth Moor, 27th March 1967.

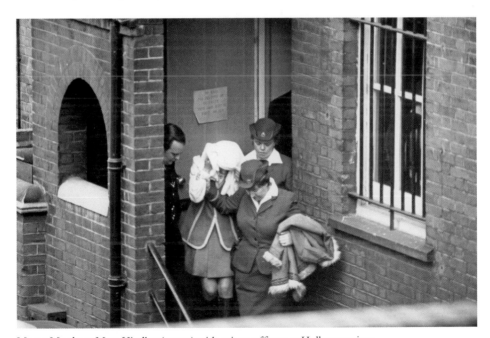

Moors Murderer Myra Hindley (centre) with prison officers at Holloway prison, London, 1st February 1974.

Police dog handlers start their search on Saddleworth Moor for the bodies of the victims killed by Ian Brady and Myra Hindley, 21st November 1986.

The media are brought up-to-date about the return to Saddleworth Moor of Ian Brady and Myra Hindley, 25th November 1986.

A police helicopter flies over Saddleworth Moor as police continue their search for the bodies of victims, 17th November 1986.

Police discover the mummified body of Pauline Reade, 20 years after she was murdered by Ian Brady and Myra Hindley. Brady is hidden from view by police at Saddleworth Moor as the discovery is made, 5th July 1987.

Moors Murderer Ian Brady with police on Saddleworth Moor, Manchester, Britain, 1987.

That same year, the council finally tore down Myra's one-time home in Hattersley. Nobody wanted to live where she and Ian had killed poor young Eddie Evans, and the neighbours were fed up with ghouls coming to stare at the house and take pictures of themselves outside it. Maybe it doesn't really make sense, but superstitions run deep. Who would sleep well in the house that had once been home to two of Britain's most notorious serial murderers?

Myra and middle age

As the 1980s drew to a close, Myra was working hard on her autobiography, intending that profits from its sale should be given to charity. Any interactions she had with the media were disappointing to her. Most journalists simply echoed the public's ongoing abhorrence of everything she had done and had come to stand for; at the same time, they were fascinated by her. Whenever they managed to dredge up something new to publish about Myra, newspaper sales would go through the roof.

Now well into middle age, Myra had become ever more religious. She joined the Franciscan order as a lay member, but they took her membership away shortly afterwards, leaving her feeling bereft and rejected. She also tried to cooperate with the ongoing search for Keith Bennett's body – or at least to give the impression of cooperating – by corresponding with his brother Alan, who had written to her privately to ask for her assistance. Alan had been just eight at the time of little Keith's disappearance. Until Myra's confession, the family had not even known for sure whether she and Ian, or some other murderer, had taken their boy.

Alan, asked by a journalist why he communicated with the woman who had killed his brother, said, 'There's no point in shouting and calling her a murdering bitch. The fact is there are only two people who know where Keith is and she is one of them - and I don't see Ian Brady helping.'

After writing to each other for a long time, Myra finally agreed to meet Alan, and he went to visit her in Durham prison. 'She took hold of my arms,' he said, 'and started crying, saying that she was sorry for all she had done, for the pain she had caused. Then we sat down and started going through the maps and things.' Myra told Alan that although she had not participated in Keith's rape and murder, she had seen him disappear ahead of her with Ian, and thought about how he looked 'like a little lamb being led to the slaughter.'

Myra finished her autobiography, but those who read it felt that it was a poor effort, maudlin about her childhood, and avoiding the real issues, the ones that everyone wanted to talk about. The whole thing read like an exercise in shifting the blame from herself. There was no indication of real remorse. Essentially, the book was unpublishable.

In 1989, Myra graduated from the Open University. A photograph of her, looking happy and handsome, was published. The response from the public was overwhelming. Nobody wanted to know about Myra finding happiness and fulfilment through her studies. If anyone had imagined that the knowledge that Myra had acquired with her time inside was to 'improve herself.' they were badly, badly wrong.

By 1990, Ian and Myra had lost whatever connection they had held onto since their incarceration. Ian published an open letter in which he referred to letters sent to him by Myra in which she referred to the murder and her role in them. Myra was aghast, because she felt that she had a chance of parole, and was actively planning to move in with Tricia, the woman with whom she had had the most serious of her relationships in prison. Then Myra met someone new, Nina Wilde, a Dutch woman who was studying criminology and who had come to Cookham Wood as part of her studies. The two women became lovers. Myra forgot about Tricia, and started planning to live instead with Nina when she was released, something that she now felt was all but inevitable. Hoping to win some support, Myra agreed to be hypnotised in an attempt to uncover lost memories that might lead searchers to Keith's remains. She also used this offer as a bargaining chip, saying that she would only be well enough to undergo hypnosis if she were allowed to see her lover, Nina.

In 1995, Myra was transferred back to Durham Jail, where she continued to work on her autobiography, and in 1998 to Highpoint, which was a medium security prison that offered considerable comfort. Here she met the priest Father Michael Teader, who heard her Confession once a week. She began to entertain the notion of being released from jail into a religious order. After all, she had been in an institution for many years. Perhaps she would do better in an all women community, focused on prayer and contemplation.

Chapter 8

Life
Means Life

Life means life

During her time in jail, Hindley had a number of lovers, including fellow prisoner Nina Wilde, and by the time of her death, she had a number of followers in the prison. Her followers were very fond of her, stating that she was cultured, well educated, supportive of them, and even defended at least one prisoner when she was attacked by another. In the prison, most agreed that Hindley was at least well behaved and worked to attain the highest command of her situation. However, not all members of the prison, or even the University she attended, felt that she could be trusted, many feeling that much of the emotion she demonstrated was carefully faked, friends chosen by their usefulness and power, and her words carefully considered before she spoke.

At one time, the British penal code was considered harsh, unyielding, and unforgiving, as the punishment for over 200 different crimes could result in death by hanging. This continued for decades, even under the attempted revamping of the law that resulted in the 1957 Homicide Act, which struggled to define murders as either capital or non-capital offences. This law still allowed hangings; death sentences for murder were believed to be the best way to deter future murderers. However, on 13 August 1964, Peter Anthony Allen and Gwynne Owen Evans would be the last two people to die in the gallows, by hanging, in England. Their crime was the incidental murder of an individual during a robbery. A number of crimes had resulted in hanging, even some when the convicted may have been innocent, and that raised concern regarding the practice of hanging.

Prime Minister Harold Wilson proposed that a modernised Britain would indeed not hang individuals, and with the support of the government, introduced legislation that led to a five-year trial period of suspended capital punishment. In 1965, The Abolition of Capital Punishment Act went into effect, against public opinion. In order to protect citizens who widely believed there would be a large increase in murders, an amendment was attached that required a second vote, an affirmative resolution, to be achieved by the first of August 1970. A second amendment attempted to determine the amount of time that could be given for imprisonment for murder, such as full-life sentences. The law remains in effect, and no people having committed a crime in Britain will be hanged. This has not always met with public approval, and quite exactly the sensationalism of crimes that followed the introduction of the abolishment of the death penalty did not gain the legislation support amongst the people. Nonetheless, no future criminals in Britain would be hanged for crimes committed and life imprisonment was instituted for severe crimes, such as murder.

The Moors Murders were a series of horrifying crimes that would seem to benefit from the abolishment of the death penalty. Ian Brady and Myra Hindley would not be hanged for their crimes, and though their initial argument was that they were indeed innocent on all counts, the death penalty could not be considered for these two, as their case was tried just a few months too late. Their crimes were beyond heinous and their attitudes completely void of remorse, and the only option was life imprisonment.

At the time of sentencing, life sentences meant that the maximum number of years the criminal would spend in prison was until their death. However, they would also receive a minimum sentence, known as a tariff, which could be designated by the Home Secretary or the judge, though later, after 2005, only judges would be able to set this amount. After the tariff is served, prisoners are evaluated at a parole hearing to determine their behaviour and level of reform, at which time they could possibly be paroled. This aspect of the abolished death penalty was by far the most frustrating to family members of the Moor's murder victims. It seemed that these two murderers, having killed five children, might one day be free to walk the streets again. Many people felt strongly that neither Brady nor Hindley should ever be considered for parole, particularly due to the still missing body of Keith Bennett.

Verdicts and Sentencing of the Moors Murderers

On 27 April 1966, Ian Brady and Myra Hindley were brought to trial at Chester Assizes, where media brought the story to the public, and waited with intensity to discover what would be the sentencing of these two criminals. During the trial, a great deal of evidence was presented, from the photographs, through the tape of the young girl's pleas for her life. The jury listened to hours of summary, deliberated for less than two hours before presenting a question to the judge, and then deliberated for just a short time after. After a trial lasting 14 days, the jury was able to reach a decision in only a couple of hours. Mr Justice Fenton Atkinson was quoted as stating that Ian Brady was guilty of 'three calculated, cool, cold-blooded murders', those of Evans, Downey, and Kilbride. His sentence for these crimes was that of three terms of life imprisonment, to which Brady had no response, no apparent remorse, and he simply walked the steps with the two prison officers. Hindley was found guilty of the same for Evans and Downey, but the verdict was not guilty in the case of Kilbride; she was held accountable for harbouring Brady, and held as an accessory after the fact. Her sentence for this verdict was life imprisonment, and she left fully composed. No remorse on the face of either, no apologies for the families they had destroyed, and no demonstration of fear or concern for where they were heading.

At that time, and when considered in many future conversations, most believed that neither Myra nor Ian should be granted tariffs of lesser time served than that of their complete life; however, in the future Myra would be considered differently, and most considered the tariff to be a 30 year minimum. Later, it would be stated that Ian Brady's tariff was 40 years, which was not acceptable to the victims' families and the greater public.

Criminal Insanity and Life Imprisonment

Ian Brady and Myra Hindley spent their first few years in prison corresponding, and even planning to marry; however, it did not last long before their ideas of the future took them too far apart to continue a relationship. Hindley was determined to see her freedom again, and Ian had accepted his fate, even making a public statement in 1978 that he would not apply for parole and that he had 'accepted the weight of the crimes both Myra and I were convicted of' and did not feel that any show of remorse would demonstrate enough change. Hindley would cease communications with Brady, and this could have been the result of the growing mental instability of Brady, or a direct result of the affair she was having with a prison officer who later would be verified as her lover.

During the first 19 years of his sentence, Brady was in mainstream prison and even developed friendships, such as with a serial poisoner with similar Nazi interests and beliefs. However, in 1985 the prison declared Brady mentally unstable, following an incident where he broke his hand punching a wall, and had him remanded to a mental hospital. It was not the first incident, as other things such as hallucinations and delusions had become a daily part of his activities in the prisons, to the point where it was believed he was not only a danger to others, but to himself as well. Some of the situations were as bizarre as believing that he could walk through walls, and others as severe as using salt to make himself violently ill. It was during this time that it was suggested that his condition might need further treatment, and he was admitted to Ashworth Hospital. Brady's first hunger strike was in 1999, and though reportedly he has been force-fed the better part of the time since, it is reported that he also does indeed feed himself, at least a little each day, while in the care of Ashworth Hospital. He would legally argue that he had a right to kill himself and refuse food, none of which supported his later tale that he was not mentally unstable.

In the Loo

While Brady seemed to get along well in his prison confinement, Hindley did not. He slowly worked his way into insanity and Ashworth Hospital, but Hindley spent a great deal of her time working on the locals in her prisons, and writing to people she thought would help her gain her freedom. Throughout all of her communications, Hindley stressed her innocence in the actual murders and rapes. This state of events continued, and in 1985, while she was in Cookham Wood, Hindley received a letter from Keith Bennett's mother, begging Hindley to help the police recover the body of her son. Hindley was aware that Brady was demonstrating mental instability, and it is believed she helped the police to garner support from the public for her next plea for freedom. She looked at pictures and a map, but insisted that she must visit the Moors if there was any chance of her finding the body.

In 1986, Detective Chief Superintendent Peter Topping, head of GMP's Criminal Investigation Department (CID), and Home

Secretary Douglas Hurd, though sceptical of the truth to Hindley's claim, determined that the visit could be productive. With many police, helicopters, and Hindley in chains, they went to determine where the final two bodies were located. They were unsuccessful, possibly in part due to the amount of attention the visit caused, and the nervousness of Hindley during the visit. However, in February 1987, Hindley confessed to Topping, Michael Fisher (her solicitor), and Reverend Peter Timms that she was involved in all five murders. More than a month later, the confession was made public, and in the 17-hour tape, which Toppings responded to and was quoted as saying he 'had witnessed a great performance rather than a genuine confession'. In addition, he 'was struck by the fact that she was never there when the killings took place. She was in the car, over the brow of the hill, in the bathroom, and even, in the case of the Evans murder, in the kitchen'. All of the tales confessed demonstrated that Hindley was not the true villain. Her activities were always by the coercion and direction of Brady, and he himself was the only one sexually abusing the victims and killing them. In every attempt, from her confession to her later letters and stories, was that she was little more than a victim herself.

Confessions and Hollin Brown Knoll

Brady was given the opportunity to also confess, when police approached him with the confession from Hindley. At first, he did not believe such a thing was possible, but after the facts, he did agree to confess if he was given the means to commit suicide immediately following it. They did not agree to this condition, and later Hindley would have a second and final visit to the Moors. Neither visits would result in the discovery of the bodies, but Hindley provided one clue that helped the search. She recalled that she could see the rocks of Hollin Brown Knoll while sitting next to Pauline Reade. This final clue would result in the body being found hardly 91.4 m from where Lesley Ann Downey was found. After confessing to Topping, Brady, too, would have his opportunity to help find the body of Keith Bennett. The search went poorly, according to Brady, due to the changes that had occurred in the Moors. While both Brady and Hindley had confessed to the knowledge of the murders of both Pauline Reade and Keith Bennett, only the body of Pauline Reade has been recovered to date.

Hindley would never confess to any other involvement in the crimes than those that set her apart from the vicious aspects of the deaths. However, later it would be suggested that Hindley and Brady had committed other crimes that they had yet to admit to, and Brady himself would supposedly confess to crimes that were unconfirmed. Brady's newest list of crimes did not match any missing persons known of, nor did the crimes result in any new bodies located. Additionally, it is strongly believed that at least Brady still knows where the body of Bennett is located, and that he may be purposefully refusing to disclose this information. No searches have been productive in locating the boy based on any information that either Brady or Hindley has supplied. Many different professionals have attempted to use the many photographs taken by Brady and Hindley of the Moors to determine where the body may be, but without success. Literally hundreds of searches have taken place, but no one has ever found any leads, and Bennett's mother passed away with no resolution.

Affairs, Escapes and Petitions

Hindley had broken off her relationship with Brady for reasons unknown, but known is that she began to work toward her freedom, and began planning her freedom with a prison officer she had fallen in love with. The first plan to gain her freedom was designed by Hindley, her lover Patricia Cairns, and Maxine Croft, a fellow inmate. The plan was to take copies of the keys to the building, including the master keys, using Camay soap. Prior to making the copies of the keys, the team had set into motion plans such as changing Myra Hindley's name to Myra Spencer and taking many pictures, with a wig, that was believed to be for passport pictures. The plan might have been successful, but for the fact that on the day that Cairns went to leave the package of the soap at London's Paddington station, to be picked up by their contact, an IRA bomb threat prevented her from leaving the package. She posted the luggage to a garage in Ilford, East London, with a set of instructions, but her contact there was suspicious of the package, for fear it was a bomb. Patricia Cairns was arrested and served time for her crime; it was Hindley's only attempt at a prison escape.

Hindley's efforts turned to seeking release through the parole board and assistance from people capable of helping reduce her tariff. She worked on self-improvement projects including reaffirmation of her religious beliefs and becoming a practising Catholic, taking University courses in the Humanities, and taking up hobbies such as pottery and badminton. She worked diligently to demonstrate her reform, and though many people believed her attempts to be acting skills of a cold and calculating criminal, others believed her attempts to demonstrate her reform warranted consideration of her case for parole. In addition, she worked hard to befriend individuals able to promote her cause, such as Lord Longford, Reverend Peter Timms, and David Astor. Others over time would also come to believe that she was reformed, but she would never be successful in her attempts at convincing the courts that she should be freed. She made three appeals against her life tariff between the years of 1997 and 2000, but the courts continuously rejected her.

During her time in jail, Hindley had a number of lovers, including fellow prisoner Nina Wilde, and by the time of her death, she had a number of followers in the prison. Her followers were very fond of her, stating that she was cultured, well educated, supportive of them, and even defended at least one prisoner when she was attacked by another. In the prison, most agreed that Hindley was at least well behaved and worked to attain the highest command of her situation. However, not all members of the prison, or even the Open University she attended, felt that she could be trusted, many feeling that much of the emotion she demonstrated was carefully faked, friends chosen by their usefulness and power, and her words carefully considered before she spoke. She had even shared her version of the events with television show producers who worked on a series that portrayed the incidents of the mid-1960s. A heavy smoker, Hindley developed angina and suffered a stroke. In November of 2002, Myra Hindley died, at age 60, of bronchial pneumonia. Though she had many supporters, it was said that more than 20 undertakers had refused to do her cremation. None of her immediate family was present at her funeral, and nearly four months after her death, a former lover scattered her ashes in Stalybridge Country Park.

Her death actually came shortly before a decision that could have changed her situation dramatically. In 2002, the Home Secretary's ability to set minimum tariffs was challenged by another prisoner with a life sentence, and represented literally hundreds of individuals in similar predicaments. Many were certain that this was finally Hindley's ability to be released, and some even began to prepare to protect her with a new identity. However, nothing would be decided until 25 November 2002, when the Law Lords determined that judges should be the only decision makers regarding minimum sentences. Part of the reasoning could have been the difficulty for politicians to represent impartial decisions when they are subject to public scrutiny in all of their actions. This change directly supported many of the arguments Hindley had raised in previous years, and if not for her death, could have rescued her from the confines in which she had spent nearly her entire life. However, it was also reasonable to believe that she may not have been released due to her involvement in the two murders that had not been charged to Brady and Hindley, or that the courts may not have believed her to be sufficiently reformed.

Release or Suicide – A Right to Die

Prior to the abolishment of capital punishment, murderers such as Brady and Hindley did not enjoy the confines of life imprisonment; they went to the gallows and were hanged in the privacy of the prison. Many people believe that this particular type of punishment was the most likely to discourage murders. Brady and Hindley were lucky, which may have been somewhat how Hindley felt, but it was in no way the feelings of Brady. On many occasions he expressed that his life or death should be his decision to make. Later, Hindley would be quoted as saying she herself felt she should have been hanged, that though she had not abused the children nor murdered them herself, her role was crucial in the their deaths. She felt that the children would never have gone willingly with Brady had she not convinced them of their safety with her. It is believed that she felt that she would have been able to confess her sins if she had been eligible for hanging. She would have confessed, and everyone would have known the truth and not the lie. Hindley would be put on suicide watch at least once during her prison sentence.

While Hindley worked hard to demonstrate the parole board should release her, Brady was also seeking release. However, his primary search for freedom was not in the attempt to be released from the prison, but a release from life. Though he would later tell the story that his insanity was just that, an attempt to be released from prison to a hospital. Over the years, it was repeated by nearly all Home Secretaries that neither Brady nor Hindley should ever be released from prison. In some cases, it was a strict case of 30 years for Hindley and 40 for Brady, but Home Secretary David Waddington, in 1990, advised Brady that he did not feel that either of them should be released, and this remained constant over the following years. Brady had determined that continuing in the direction of Hindley would not be his path, and he proceeded to appear to be insane during many interactions with staff members in each location he was held.

In 1999, the High Court determined that Brady did not have the right to starve himself, and that suicide was unacceptable. His appeal was later denied as well, stating that he was not refusing medical services, and that force feeding did not constitute a service he could refuse. He was force fed using a feeding tube, and this continued for many years; he even sported this particular item at his hearing in June 2013, when he demanded that the court release him back to prison. His attempts at suicide were primarily only by starvation, though his appearance has never been reported to signify that he had made much progress. While his sincerity in this manner can be questioned, he had begun refusing medications for his condition in 2000, and in 2006, he attempted to receive paracetamol tablets from a woman who attempted to smuggle them inside a book to him. He was unable to retrieve these, which would have been a lethal dose, and no similar attempts are known.

During the hearing, held per the demand of Brady, the objective was to understand if Brady suffered a condition that warranted his return to the prison. Dr Grounds described Brady as suffering from paranoid narcissism, which is understood to include 'superiority, self-centeredness, contempt, [and] hostility'. Meanwhile, Dr Collins has already defined Brady as 'handicapped by his mental disorder' and suggested that he might attempt suicide in the prison. In the past, Brady had even suggested that he was 'controlled by external things' and he had had long conversations with individuals who were not in the room with him. When asked if Brady would kill himself if permitted to return to prison, Brady refused to answer, and suggested that it was not the business of anyone if this were to be the case. He continued to explain that his conditions were not real, and that he had used method acting to lead the doctors to the conclusions they had used to diagnose him. However, during the hearing, Brady was not able to remain clear in his responses, wandering in his communications, and occasionally demonstrating an inability to answer questions with clear answers. Brady is currently 75 years old, and continues to serve out his sentence at Ashworth Hospital.

Not only was the hearing another example of the difficulty Brady currently has in remaining lucid in his conversations, but it also demonstrated a strange desire to further enrage public opinion. He stated that the murders he had committed were simply 'an existential exercise'; in some ways, it seemed he was nearly suggesting the entire thing was just a game, or some joke like might occur when you hide a friend's mobile phone or hang a sister's doll from the ceiling fan. This very remark was intended to increase the likelihood that he would be placed back into the prison for his heinous crimes. During the tribunal, it was unclear if he was indeed always faking his mental condition, or if his mental condition had taken on this new capacity of control. Nothing that was admitted at the time of the tribunal identified him as without a mental handicap, or able to be trusted not to make any continued suicide attempts. He was refused his release to a prison, and remains under watch for suicide attempts.

Truth and Lies

Over the years, Hindley maintained her innocence, and although she knew of, and contributed to the deaths of the five children, she herself had neither sexually abused them, nor had she been present at the abuse and murders. However, Brady told quite a different story regarding Hindley's involvement in the crimes. He proceeded to write that she was indeed involved, and that her involvement was out of love for him. He warned that she was of the habit of telling people exactly what they wanted to hear to be pleased with her, accusing her of being a chameleon, and suggesting that she also contributed to at least the killings as well. He felt that Hindley demonstrated 'destructive delusion' in her suggestion that he was completely to blame, and that he had forced or coerced her into the activities, particularly in her suggestions that he had drugged or blackmailed her. In some conversations, Brady would suggest that Hindley even acted in the sexual abuse and rapes of the children. However, unlike others who have suggested that Hindley has admitted to murders unknown at this time, Brady has not suggested in many years that other crimes were committed.

While Hindley would spend time writing to television show producers, Brady would spend time writing. Hindley's work with the producers caused a great deal of negative publicity and outrage from the parents of the murdered children. Similarly, Brady's book, *The Gates of Janus*, caused outrage at the thought that he could earn as much as £12,000 for the book. The book, published by Feral House in the U.S., was a book about serial killers, rather than a book about his killings, and in the book, he attempted to explain the way a serial killer thinks, rather than give any evidence to his own activities. However, Colin Wilson, a criminologist believed to have convinced Brady to write the book, noted that Brady does have an autobiography written and ready for publication upon his death. Numerous people believe that the autobiography will provide police with the location of Keith Bennett's body, and some believe it will detail other murders that the two have not previously confessed to during their years.

As Hindley never wrote anything that suggested she was anything other than innocent in the crimes, it is unlikely that anything written by Brady will change the mind of Hindley supporters. Over the years it has been suggested that neither was innocent, and that both suffered a different psychological defect that when united through contact created the volatile couple's behaviour. However, it is not known if the murders would not have occurred if they had not met. The autobiography could shed light on some of the activities between the two, or even to the history that led Brady to the crimes. Additionally, many people who did not feel that Hindley was innocent of the crimes, or coerced by the supposedly charming Brady, are extremely interested to find out exactly what role Brady will say Hindley played in the crimes. It is likely that the book may not even exist, or that if it does, it continues with more of the confused stories and misleading accusations that are most recently the normal conversations of Brady, as demonstrated in his tribunal. Regardless of what the autobiography says, if there is one, it is unlikely that the full truth will ever be known.

Prior to the abolishment of capital punishment, murderers such as Brady and Hindley did not enjoy the confines of life imprisonment; they went to the gallows and were hung in the privacy of the prison. Many people believe that this particular type of punishment was the most likely to discourage murders. Brady and Hindley were lucky, which may have been somewhat how Hindley felt, but it was in no way the feelings of Brady. On many occasions he expressed that his life or death should be his decision to make. Later, Hindley would be quoted as saying she herself felt she should have been hanged, that though she had not abused the children nor murdered them herself, her role was crucial in the their deaths. She felt that the children would never have gone willingly with Brady had she not convinced them of their safety with her. It is believed that she felt that she would have been able to confess her sins if she had been eligible for hanging. She would have confessed, and everyone would have known the truth and not the lie. Hindley would be put on suicide watch at least once during her prison sentence.

Chapter 9

Hindley Dies

Hindley Dies

Myra had also instructed that her organs should not be made available for donation upon her death – perhaps not considering the fact that nobody would be likely to want to receive a donation from such a hated character.

Throughout her long incarceration, Myra never gave up on her dream of one day being free. However, as she grew older, her health began to fail. Despite her outward appearance of robustness and strength, by her mid-fifties, Myra was frail. In December 1999, a close friend of hers, Father Bert White, was killed in a car crash. She was desperately upset. Possibly the shock contributed to her collapse shortly afterwards.

Under a false name, Myra was admitted to Addenbrooke's Hospital in Cambridge, where it was discovered she had had a cerebral aneurysm, which meant that one of the arteries inside her brain had become swollen. This is a dangerous condition, and Myra was under no illusions as to the risks and dangers. She made it clear that should she slip into a coma at some future point, she did not wish to be resuscitated. However, she responded well to treatment and was able to return to prison.

Myra had been advised by her doctors to give up smoking, but she refused; smoking gave her great pleasure, and with the monotony of prison life, she deserved it.

Presumably believing that it would lend credibility to her quest to leave prison, Myra collaborated with filmmaker Duncan Staff on 'Modern Times', a film about her relationship with Ian, and the murders they carried out together. A reviewer commented afterwards on the 'yawning discrepancy between the cold facts, and Hindley's recollection of them'. Even after all these years, Myra was refusing to face up to the reality of what she had done. She continued to parrot the story of herself as the hapless young girl who was powerless to resist Ian's charms. The only comment that rang true, the reviewer said, was when Myra sadly remarked the she would have been better off being hanged.

On 30 March 2000, just a month after the film was aired, Myra lost yet another bid for freedom; she had taken her fight to the European courts. She was desperately disappointed. She also asked permission to make a compassionate visit to Nellie, her mother, and this was also turned down. Perhaps these disappointments had an impact on her health, because a year later she was once again sent to hospital.

As Myra's health continued to deteriorate, the family of Keith Bennett were painfully aware that they were going to lose their slender chance of finding out where her victim lay. She was no longer well enough to visit the moor herself, so she was sent photographs and maps, in the hope that they would prompt her memory and perhaps prick her conscience.

In 2001, two of Myra's longest champions died, Lord Longford and David Astor, the editor of The Observer. Both had long insisted that Myra was rehabilitated, and deserved consideration for parole. They had often pointed out that other killers had been considered for parole after fewer years in prison, and that she was apparently being singled out for special treatment. These losses, too, were a body blow for Myra's already compromised health and strength. Her weight became extremely volatile, and she became ever more reclusive.

By the autumn of 2002, Myra was on a vast array of medications to treat her asthma, heart condition, osteoporosis and osteoarthritis, as well as a number of psychological conditions including insomnia and depression. She did not appear to have the will to fight any of her health conditions, and had pretty much given up. In November she developed a nasty chest infection and was prescribed antibiotics, but shortly afterwards she was admitted to hospital in Bury St Edwards, struggling to breathe. She managed to instruct the doctors that she should not be resuscitated if her heart gave out, or if she became completely unable to breathe. Myra had also instructed that her organs should not be made available for donation upon her death – perhaps not considering the fact that nobody would be likely to want to receive a donation from such a hated character.

Myra Draws Her Final Breath

Myra grew progressively sicker, and on November 16, after four days in hospital, she became deeply distressed. It was evident that she was nearing the end. Her priest was called and gave her the last rites. She briefly became conscious enough to talk about her mother, and then she was gone. She was just sixty years old – young to die, by the standards of today. Afterwards, her priest, Father Michael, said:

She slipped quietly from a world still raging against her. She wasn't afraid of death. It held no fears for her. Why should it? God doesn't have any favourites: he doesn't say, I'll forgive that sin but not that one, and I'll forgive you and not you. That's my belief and I tried to instil that in Myra before she died.

After her death, everything that had been in Myra's hospital room, as well as the bedding and furniture, was burnt. It was unthinkable that anyone else might lay their head where Britain's most hated woman had had her final repose. While this makes no rational sense, the visceral hatred with which most people think of Myra Hindley, child killer, makes it more than understandable.

After her death

Myra's death unleashed a new wave of interest in her life and crimes. The News of the World led with a story under the blaring headline, 'Myra Hindley in Hell'. The press raked over every aspect of her life, and marvelled at how the story of Manchester's female serial killer had remained alive through her long years of incarceration, and had even thrived in some respects, and enjoyed life. She had earned a degree at the Open University and she had had friends and lovers. She had been behind bars, but it had not always been bad for her. In some ways, she had managed to leave her tough working class roots behind her.

While much of the media commentary focused on her characterisation as a 'monster', some of the commentators focused instead on what they had seen as her rehabilitation, and the woman she had become in middle age. In The Guardian, her obituary described her as 'warm, funny and blunt, unrecognisable as the Gorgon who haunted parents' imaginations.'

For the Bennett family, Myra's death was a great blow – not because they had the slightest sympathy for her, but because now they felt sure that they would never learn where Keith was buried. Ian Brady was never going to talk; Myra had been their last and only hope.

Myra had loomed so large in the lives of the bereaved that it was hard for them to believe that she was really gone. John Kilbride's brother Danny said that his first reaction was that it wasn't really true; that she had been released in secret, and the story of her death had been fabricated. He was not alone in this belief. In fact, the Internet was abuzz with conspiracy theorists, who pointed to the fact that Myra had had her supporters. A story of a supposed sighting of Myra, alive and well, did the rounds of the Internet forums, and to this day, there are those who believe that Myra's death and the subsequent funeral were an elaborate hoax, designed to provide Britain's most hated woman with the freedom she craved.

The truth, of course, was more banal. Myra died and was cremated. A burial was out of the question – any grave where she lay would surely be defaced or, worse, visited by ghouls and would be copycat killers.

Myra's body was placed in a chipboard coffin with a pine veneer on top; someone who had loved her had paid for an arrangement of red roses and lilies to be placed on top. There were other flowers, too. A service was held at a crematorium near Cambridge, with massive police security – a security team searched everywhere before the service, in case there had been any attempt at a terrorist attack of some sort.

As she had been ill for some time, Myra had given her funeral a great deal of thought. She had asked for Albinoni's Adagio, one of the pieces played at Princess Diana's funeral in 1997, to be played when her coffin arrived, but her request was not granted. Instead she was brought into the crematorium to the blaring sound of the lorries passing by on the A14.

Banks of cameras and journalists watched the scene behind the steel barriers that had been erected and under the harsh electric lights that were powered by noisy generators. Nellie, who was 82 years old, was not well enough to attend her daughter's funeral, which featured just a few people – Myra's solicitors, and the freedom campaigner Trisha Forrester, and Myra's friend and confessor, Father Michael, who sprinkled holy water on her coffin. None of the women who had been Myra's lovers in prison were there.

The funeral mass, which had been requested by Myra and paid for with her savings, lasted just twenty-five minutes and then the coffin entered the incinerator. The policeman overseeing the proceedings, Superintendent Raine, told the gathered reporters that her ashes would be handed over to the prison service, and given by them to Myra's family members.

After the funeral, David Smith was interviewed. He told the journalist that he felt nothing, no emotion whatsoever, when he heard that Myra had died and was gone. 'But on the night she was cremated,' he said, 'I had a feeling that something good was happening. They were burning her and that meant that there wasn't a place on this earth that she will be. She is dust; she's not even in the air. She has gone off this planet and finally, she is nothing.'

David expressed his regret that Myra and Ian had not faced the death penalty for their crimes, and stressed his view that, of the two of them, Myra was by far the worst: 'She was the most evil. Brady had the decency to have himself certified mad and, whether he is or not, it is comforting to presume he is... He didn't stalk the streets, offering kiddies sweeties. She did, knowing what the children were wanted for, knowing that they would get into the car with her, a woman, and knowing they wouldn't go with a man.'

It was reported that Myra's ashes were scattered four months later by one of her former lovers, in Stalybridge Country park less than ten miles away from the moors where she and Ian and buried their victims.

Nellie, Myra's mother, died about a year later. She had lived as a recluse, even in her nursing home, afraid that people would find out whose mother she was, and take it out on her.

David Smith, whose entire adult life had been sullied by his earlier friendship with Ian and Myra, and whose first marriage had been poisoned by the association, died in May 2012. He had eventually found peace in a remote area of Connemara, Ireland, where the locals accepted him as he was. David and his second wife ran a guest house and lived a peaceful, quiet life in the wilds of western Ireland. All his life David had suffered flashbacks and panic attacks about the moment he had seen Eddie Evans take his last breath. In 1969, he had served time in prison when he lashed out at someone who had attacked him repeatedly, accusing him of being involved with the murders. David had struggled to keep a job, as people had often walked off their jobs or picked a fight with him when he was hired to work somewhere. In prison, he had had to be housed with the sexual offenders for his own safety. Maureen left him while he was in prison – they had three sons by then. On his release in 1971, he met Mary, who gave birth to a daughter, Jodie, two years later. It was hard for Mary – David's children were all regularly bullied, they couldn't go out, and every single time Ian and Myra appeared in the newspapers, bricks were thrown through their living room window. At one stage, the boys' pet rabbits were killed. David was determined for a long time not to move. He had not done anything wrong. In fact, if he hadn't gone to the police, Myra and Ian would have been free to go on killing.

Winnie Johnson, Keith Bennett's mother, died on 18 August 2012. She had lived for all those years without knowing where her little boy had been buried. A pair of Keith's glasses was placed in the coffin with her, and the Kilbride family, which had shared so much of her sorrow, sent a floral tribute. She was remembered as a woman who had lived with her grief with great dignity, but who had gone to her grave with the weight of her sorrow. Ian and Myra could at any point have given her the comfort that she craved, and the opportunity to provide her little boy with a Christian funeral. Perhaps they found some pleasure in the knowledge that at least one of their crimes had been 'the perfect murder.'

Since Myra and Ian were imprisoned for their deeds, other serial killers have been apprehended, some of whom killed even more people. None has captured the imagination like Myra, whose peroxide blonde locks and panda eyes are still the stuff of nightmares.

Conspiracy of Hindley's Death

To this day, some believe that Hindley was finally able to gather enough supporters to have her wish granted freedom and a new identity. Conspiracy is suggested to have occurred by faking her death. Myra Hindley was reported to have died on the 15th of November 2002, at age 60, from a chest infection, which was aggravated by her heart condition and other health issues already, plaguing her. Her death came after what was believed by the press to be a heart attack approximately two weeks prior, and she had been hospitalised since the 12th due to her current illness. Her inquest did not include any family members, and according to authorities, the small inquest was designed to prevent media involvement and to increase the likelihood that it would be completed quickly, as the death was believed to be of natural causes. The inquest, on January 23rd of 2003, was unanimous, the jury consisted of eight women and three men and was concluded in 48 minutes, with the decision that Myra Hindley had died of natural causes, specifically bronchial pneumonia, accompanied with hypertension and coronary heart disease. This was also the report by Peter Dean, whom had received the account from Dr Michael Heath, regarding Hindley's death. Her death came as no surprise to doctors because they stated she had been a very heavy smoker who had already suffered from a number of conditions that were heralding in her end.

The post mortem was done at West Suffolk Hospital, following her death, which was listed by hospital staff as caused by complications from bronchial pneumonia and was aggravated by her heart problems. In addition, the hospital reported that she was taking medications for multiple conditions, including bronchitis, angina, osteoporosis, cholesterol, asthma, and other things such as insomnia. This information supports her cause of death. It is believed that her condition was also worsened due to her high blood pressure and her blocked arteries, which had caused previous problems with her heart and had caused her to be considered sickly and hospitalised on other occasions.

The sudden and swift cremation, on the 20th of November 2002 was believed to be part of the conspiracy as it occurred very swiftly and in secret. However, the funeral was attended by twelve people, her lawyers, Father Michael Teader – her priest, as well as her niece

The funeral of Pauline Reade, young victim of Ian Brady and Myra Hindley, 8th August 1987.

Ian Brady is held at Ashworth Secure Hospital (prison), 1995.

Winnie Johnson, mother of Moor's Murder victim Keith Bennett, demonstrating outside Wandsworth Prison, London, 5th April 1998.

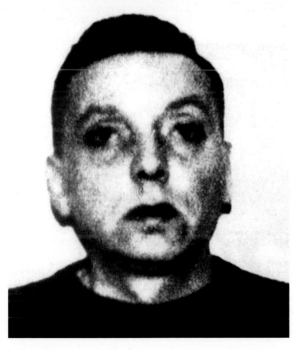

A more recent photograph of Ian Brady before he went on hunger strike in an attempt to end his life, 2000.

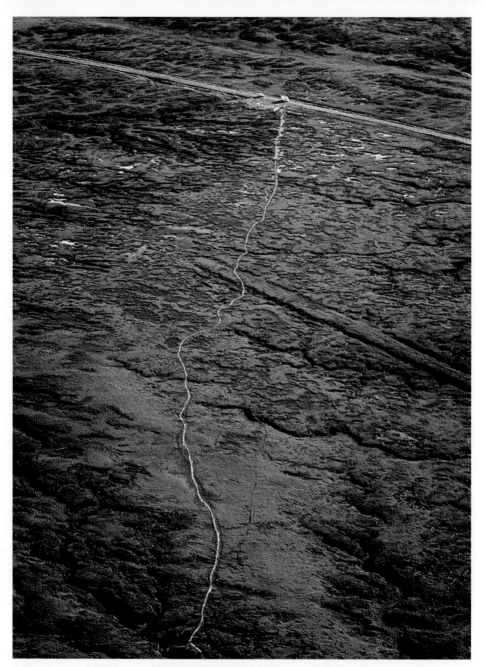

An aerial view of Saddleworth Moor, North East of Manchester. A yellow rope marks a path from the road to Shiny Brook, where Moors Murderer Myra Hindley claims that the body of Keith Bennett is buried, 13th November 2001.

The funeral of Myra Hindley takes place in Cambridge, 20th November 2002.

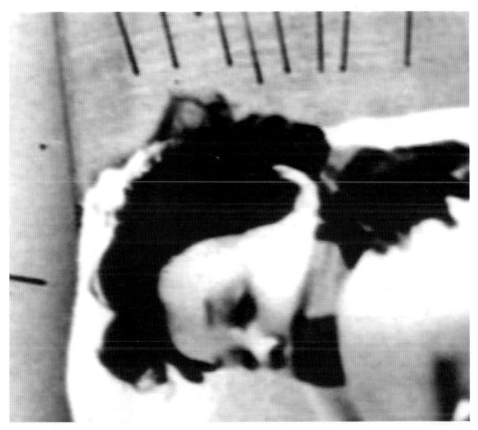

A photograph of Moor's Murder victim Lesley Ann Downey, aged 10, bound and gagged by Ian Brady and Myra Hindley.

A photograph of Lesley Ann Downey, aged 10.

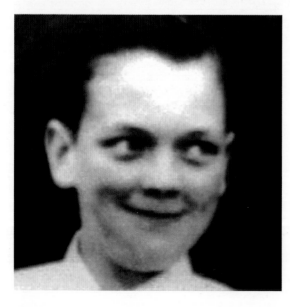

A photograph of John Kilbride,
aged 12, victim of Moor's Murderers
Ian Brady and Myra Hindley.

Officers from Greater Manchester Police search Saddleworth Moor for the body of Keith
Bennett, the only known victim of Ian Brady and Myra Hindley still not found, 1st July 2009.

Ashworth Hospital in Merseyside, where Ian Brady is held, 17th August 2012.

Unmarked tributes by a dirt track off Wessenden Head Road on Saddleworth Moor, 17th August 2012.

Unmarked tributes near Saddleworth Moor, in memory of the victims of
Ian Brady and Myra Hindley, 17th August 2012.

and brother-in-law. These were also to be decision makers regarding where her ashes would be scattered later. This secrecy and problems factored in with the closed method of the inquest brought many people to wonder regarding her actual death. Furthermore, the identity of the deceased was confirmed by a fingerprint expert with the Suffolk Police, Graham Cook, who said it was beyond doubt that the prints of the deceased matched those taken from Myra Hindley in October of 1965. This did not prevent other people from suggesting this was not the case, and that her death was faked. It was also well supported by the fact that over her many years, Hindley had gained powerful supporters such as Lord Longford.

Many people were greatly concerned that she had gathered more supporters who were able to help her escape her life of imprisonment and provide her with a secret identity to serve her outside of the prison. This was not unsupported, as Myra Hindley's medical records were also filed under a false name that of Christine Charlton, and her family had received new names to help protect them from the abuse associated with being related to a mass murderer. Additionally, in a previous attempt at escape she had been set up with a new identity. Much of the problem occurred as a direct result of the management of her death and the secrecy, which was used to both cremate and rid the location of any of the associated items that could be taken as souvenirs. The authorities spoke of difficulty in finding funeral directors willing to work with Myra Hindley's body due to the degree of public hatred of her. Paired with the risk of theft of property due to an interest in people to take articles they believed to belong to Myra or any items that may have touched her at the time of her death, was suggested as accounting for the secrecy and the complications surrounding Hindley's death.

This is not to suggest that the Prison Service or those involved with the resulting incidents were strictly participating in a conspiracy, but it does support that the conspiracy occurred. Every effort was taken to prevent there being any reason for collectors to further harass the hospital following her death, and furthermore the removal of any evidence prevented later patients from feeling uncomfortable. This was the same thought behind the cleaning of the crematory and this removed any chance of DNA being found later. As no evidence exists demonstrating that Hindley died on that day, no confirmation can be given that truly counters the statements of the conspiracy. Additionally, an inmate in prison just before she was admitted to hospital, said that Hindley did not appear to be unwell. She further stated that Hindley had recently had her hair permed and styled. Many of Hindley's supporters, including Father Michael Teader, were strong believers that she had changed, and that she had only committed the crimes as part of an unholy control that Brady had over her in her younger years. They most typically also believed that she herself had not done any of the molesting nor the actual murders. Her supporters had petitioned often for her release, based on the fact that she had indeed reformed and that she had spent more time in prison than any other murderer to date. While this set of circumstances led many people to suggest she had not actually died of any causes on the 15th, it would not be until further evidence would be brought to light that more people would come to believe this conspiracy theory.

Approximately six weeks following the death of Myra Hindley, a primary school nurse believed herself to come into direct contact with the woman. The nurse explained to police and to a friend that she had been driving along a country land when she was hit by a car from behind. Exiting the car she approached the other drive and exclaimed, "Oh my God you're Myra Hindley," to which the other driver burst into tears and answered only "you can't say that, you can't say that" and immediately got back into her car and drove away. Later the nurse explained that she had called the police and informed them of her experience, only to be told that she must withdraw her accident claim and report. She was informed that she should insist the incident had never happened; however, she had already told a friend, who had shared the story with a journalist she knew. The journalist worked for a media outlet that typically accepts stories of this type, a major tabloid paper, which is not listed in any of the media coverage of the story. However, the tabloid would not release the story, stating that it had to be buried, and no further explanation was given. Strangely, just a short time later, a new story was published, which announced that the ashes of Hindley had been discovered in the Moors, and this story was promoted widely throughout the media.

As a conspiracy, it holds qualities of truth, in that in previous attempts to be freed, whether by escape or through parole, Hindley had talked of becoming a missionary or a nun to embrace religion. In addition, her previous lover had also been a nun, and a Catholic priest who reportedly gave Myra Hindley her final rites at 4:55 am, on the day of her death. A Catholic priest had converted Hindley to Catholicism, and the car incident was only six miles from his residence and a local convent. The priest, Father Michael Teader, was also the beneficiary of the proceeds remaining to Hindley at the time of her death; along with a number of charities who reportedly have not, all received the stated amounts. Additionally, Father Michael Teader reported that he was tasked with finding a final resting place for Hindley, and that he should have selected the location of the crimes seems almost unlikely. This decision would not specifically require the permission or consent of the family, though he stated he would confer with the family prior to selecting her final resting place.

It was not enough that she had died peacefully and with a priest at her side, much in contrast to the deaths of the victims she and Brady had brutally murdered, but the thought that she might live her remaining years, into old age, in some peaceful convent leaves many people both concerned and angry. While not all people believe her to still be alive at this current time, many people believe she was at least still alive until October of 2011, and living in the convent nearby where the primary school nurse states the accident had occurred. As all evidence of the death of Hindley has been scrubbed away, from sheets and hospital rooms through the furnace where she was cremated, and though her ashes were said to be found, no materials that can be tested for DNA have been admitted for study. In addition, everything that occurred since the time of her reported death had been meticulously prepared, including thank you notes to the funeral director.

To further complicate the conditions around Hindley's death, initial stories and reports were often contradictory, with everything from who attended her funeral to information about when her ashes had been scattered. Many people believe that the world's hatred of Hindley could have resulted in her removal from prison under the conditions of conspiracy, because unlike many other criminals, she would not be able to be granted any type of reprieve and all of her supporters believed she had been truly reformed. Not only were her supporters moved by the changes believed to be seen in her, but Hindley impressed researchers who pointed to her perceived reform as an example that prison terms worked. This was not true in the case of Brady, who to this day does not believe his actions were wrong or deserved punishment.

Whether Hindley lives today, or if her ashes are scattered in the Moors, or at Stalybirdge Country Park as claimed, she will live on in the memories of all people for many years. She represented something that most people could not have fathomed, a woman willing to aide or contribute to the abduction, molestation, rape, and brutal murder of children. In history, her actions will remain, and though since this incident other vicious murderers, including females, have come to serve justice by their time in prison, Hindley was the first and her situation was long sensationalised in the media during her life, and even after her life was believed to be extinguished.

Women around the world still hate her, hate what she represents, and hate what she allowed to occur. Some people still hate her most because they knew her, and had risked the lives of their children by living near to her or by allowing her to spend time with their own children. While some people also believe she was a victim, most agree that she represents the worst in all people, and is an example of the cruelty we do not expect of women.

As a conspiracy, it holds qualities of truth, in that in previous attempts to be freed, whether by escape or through parole, Hindley had talked of becoming a missionary or to nun and embrace religion. In addition, her previous lover had also been a nun, and the Catholic priest who reportedly gave Myra Hindley her final rites at 4:55 am, on the day of her death. A Catholic priest had converted Hindley to Catholicism, and the car incident was only six miles from his residence and a local convent. The priest, Father Michael Teader, was also the beneficiary of the proceeds remaining to Hindley at the time of her death; along with a number of charities who reportedly have not, all received the stated amounts.

Chapter 10

Myra and Ian's Letters from Behind Bars

Myra and Ian's Letters from Behind Bars

After the sentencing, Myra and Ian started their life sentences, never to see each other again. They still wrote avidly, however, and worked hard at keeping their relationship going despite what seemed to be insuperable odds. They had accepted that Ian would probably never see the outside world again. They both started to study German — the language of the Nazis whom they both admired so much — and sent each other hints and compared exam results in their letters. Myra proved to be a superior student. When she got an A in her O-level, which she managed to sit before Ian, he wrote to her to tell her how proud he was of her achievements.

Despite the setback of being found guilty and sent to jail, Myra and Ian still lived very much in a fantasy world in which they were special people, better than anyone else and they still felt very much in love with each other. Even though they were confined in different prisons, far away from each other, they remained in close contact, writing to each other continuously — after all, the one thing they had plenty of now was time!

Even before they had been sent to prison, Myra and Ian had devoted a lot of time before capture in creating a special handwriting code that enabled them to put their sick sexual fantasies into writing, which when separated could be deciphered to help them share the sick thrills individually and help them come to life. At one stage, Ian managed to give her a notebook that he had filled with stories written in code – all of them were about hurting children. A code to deciphering the stories was provided on a separate piece of paper. Back in her cell, Myra pored over the notes, and copied them into an exercise book, thinly disguised as poetry, and interspersed with real poems. One of the notes read, "Why don't you throw acid on Brett?" Brett was the little brother of Lesley Ann Downey.

It was unsurprising that the prison authorities did not intercept the code. It was simple, but elegant. First of all, both Myra and Ian dated their letters. If the date was underlined, it meant that the letter contained a message. The code always began six lines into the letter, and the seventh and eighth words began the message. From then on, the message was contained in the seventh and eight words of every other line. The letter referring to Brett (including correct end of lines) read like this:

"I've been thinking for a while, why don't you ask if you can go to church on Sundays so we can at least see each other there? It's your right to go there. You get some one to help with this. See the Governor if necessary. There are places in the chapel for people in your situation Ian, so ask

someone to look into it for you. There's someone here who goes with two officers. She's in here for killing her own child and also for attempting to throw acid in her boyfriend's face. No-one likes her; she's on Rule 43 of course. Re; your mention of facial expressions in your last letter, I, too, wish I could have seen the one on Brett. His face was a picture when you stared him out!"

Myra's reason for writing these letters was a straightforward one. Ian had asked her to send her things that would excite him, and he had provided her with a list of subjects that she could write about. Apparently, he had provided her with the list of subjects in alphabetical order, as organised as he had been when they were planning and carrying out the murders. In the outside world, although Myra and Ian had had an active sex life, normal sex had never been enough for him; he had always had to engage in violent fantasies in order to feel satisfied. Now in prison, his need to share his sick imagination must have been all the greater. Lucky for him, then, that Myra remained eager and ready to oblige. Both Myra and Ian had good writing skills and very active imaginations. They were more than able to come up with ways of eluding censorship and bringing each other the sordid tales and memories they needed to feel satisfied. By sharing these messages and the sick fantasies they contained, Myra and Ian were able to feel that they were still together, in a way. They were still lovers, whose hearts beat as one.

Myra and Ian's Letters from Behind Bars

After the sentencing, Myra and Ian started their prison life, never to see each other again. They still wrote avidly, however, and worked hard at keeping their relationship going despite what seemed to be insuperable odds. They had accepted that Ian would probably never see the outside world again. They both started to study German – the language of the Nazis whom they both admired so much – and sent each other hints and compared exam results in their letters. Myra proved to be a superior student. When she got an A in her O-level, which she managed to sit before Ian, he wrote to her to tell her how proud he was of her achievements.

All the while, they still exchanged messages, using the agreed secret code that Ian had devised, about hurting children. Often, despite the code, these messages were not very explicit. Frequently even a slight reference to a secret that they shared about something they had done together was enough to bring to the fore the details of one of their hideous escapades.

Myra often wrote to Ian with a very girlish tone.

"Dearest Ian," she wrote,

"hello my hairy little gerkilchin, It was with profound relief I received your letter today… it was a lovely, soothing, nostalgic letter which comforted me almost as if you were here yourself.

I had a beautifully tender dream about you last night and awoke feeling safe and secure, thinking I was in the harbour of your arms…

I pictured your face and said your name to myself over and over and imagined the arms of the chair I was clenching to be your hands, lovely strong "insurance" hands (remember?) Freedom without you means nothing.

I've got one interest in life and that's you. We had six short but precious years together, six years of memories to sustain us until we're together again, to make dreams realities."

In their letters, Myra and Ian did not mention the murders directly very often, but in one of her letters Myra quipped, "I didn't murder any moors, did you?" referring to the nickname the press had quickly coined for them: "The Moors Murderers."

Myra and Ian felt very aggrieved by the fact that they were not entitled to conjugal visits. They wanted to be considered common-law spouses and be given the right to see each other occasionally, but this was always rejected.

Rejection Of Her Master

Myra was fascinated in prison when she realised that many of the prisoners had lesbian relationships with each other. In most cases, the women were not really lesbians by inclination – it was a case of "making do." Strong relationships formed and at night, when the lights were out, lovers would often call to each other from one cell to the next. Myra wrote about of all this in her letters to Ian, which must have been very titillating for him. In their letters, Myra and Ian also speculated about how they might one day be able to escape.

Myra and Ian corresponded for a total of six and a half years before finally agreeing to stop. The romance was over. Their relationship, now conducted entirely in writing, finally ended when she started a love relationship with Trish, the prison warder who would be her lover for many years. At this point, Myra finally wrote to her mother to ask her to send Ian a photograph album that he had been asking for a long time (containing mostly landscape photographs of the moors, presumably it would remind him of the murders and bring him pleasure in his lonely cell) and then to Ian, to end their relationship.

Although Myra was sure that she was in love with Trish, and knew that ending the relationship with Ian was the right thing to do, it was difficult for her to write that final letter. They had shared so much, after all. Somehow, she managed to write it and get it in the post.

Ian was absolutely furious when he received Myra's letter. Although he must have picked up from her correspondence that there had been a shift in her feelings for him, seeing this written down in black and white was devastating for him. They had both clung to the idea that one day Myra would be released from prison and that then she would be able to visit him and write to him about her experiences in the outside world. This had been the vision that had sustained them both. Although Myra had told Ian that their relationship was over, he continued to write. Determined to commit herself to her new relationship, she returned her letters unopened, and burned all her correspondence with him with the help of her lover, Trish.

Brady Turns On Myra

Until this point, Myra's letters had been a lifeline to Ian along with the notion that one day she would be free and would be in a position to write to him about her exciting life on the outside. In return, Ian had done his best to be protective of Myra, going along with the idea that he had been the main instigator of the crimes, and she had simply been his accomplice. Only by presenting Myra as the junior partner to his crimes could either of them hope that one day she would be released.

But now that Myra had broken off their relationship and indicated that she would not be writing again, despite his repeated pleas that she reconsider, Ian was absolutely furious. He decided that Myra had betrayed him and that now she deserved whatever she got. Whereas he had previously been very protective towards her, now he released all his venom on her and decided that he would portray her as what she had always been; very much an active partner in their crimes, a vicious, dangerous and complex woman who deserved to be given every punishment that he had received, and more.

And when Hindley ended their connection, he said that she was a manipulative liar and as evil as him. Betrayed, he plotted his revenge. As this was all taking place in the context of Myra's appeals for release, he had plenty of scope. Although Myra had burned his letters to her, Ian knew that her letters to him were filled with ammunition against her, and sent his solicitor, Benedict Birnberg, all the correspondence she had sent him before the trial.

In 1997 Ian Brady sent a damning letter to the Home Office in which he made reference to Myra corresponding with him whilst in Prison. The letter was sent to the then Home Secretary, Jack Straw and appears below, although three sections are removed due to legal restrictions.

Dear Sir,

Despite having contributed a brief factual statement, dated 31st Oct 97 (copy enclosed), to the Home Secretary in the continuing annual debate re whether my co-defendant, Myra Hindley, should be released, commentators and journalists still press me for further elucidation.

The answers to the variegated questions put are discoverable in the aggregate three decades of copious public and official files, though no individual has yet possessed the necessary acumen to interpret them with comprehensive accuracy and consistency. Therefore, I'll concisely clarify, reductio ad absurdum, some of the additional pertinent questions posed, avoiding the legal, moral and theological sophism of others.

(1) The pivotal factor of our relationship. First accept the determinant. Myra Hindley and I once loved each other. We were a unified force, not two conflicting entities. The relationship was not based on the delusional concept of folie a deux, but on a conscious/subconscious emotional and psychological affinity. She regarded periodic homicides as rituals of reciprocal innervation, marriage ceremonies theoretically binding us ever closer. As the records show, before we met my criminal activities had been primarily mercenary. Afterwards, a duality of motivation developed. Existential philosophy melded with the spirituality of death and became predominant. We experimented with the concept of total possibility. Instead of the requisite Lady Macbeth, I got Messalina. Apart our futures would have taken radically divergent courses.

(2) The reason why the trial judge made a distinction between Myra Hindley and myself. Before entering the witness box, I instructed both her counsel and my own to ask me specific questions designed to give the fullest opportunity of providing a cover for Myra. This managed to get her off on one murder charge. I also told her to adopt a distancing strategy when she went into the witness box, admitting to minor crimes whilst denying major. When, upon my advice, she appealed against sentence on the grounds that she should have been tried separately, Lord Chief Justice Parker denied the appeal, stating that, far from being disadvantaged by being tried with me,

it had been to her great benefit as all my evidence had been in her favour.

For twenty years I continued to ratify the cover I had given her at the trial whilst, in contrast, she systematically began to fabricate upon it to my detriment. Therefore, when I learned from the Panorama programme this week that she was now claiming I had threatened to kill her if she did not participate in the Moors murders, I considered that the lowest lie of all. The fact that she continued to write several lengthy letters a week to me for seven years after we were imprisoned contradicts this cynical allegation.

Perhaps her expedient demonomania now implies that I exercised an evil influence over her for seven years from my prison cell three-hundred miles distant? In character she is essentially a chameleon, adopting whatever camouflage will suit and voicing whatever she believes the individual wishes to hear. This subliminal soft-sell lured the innocent and naive. As for the parole board, I advised her to build on three pillars: educational studies, powerful contacts and religion. She did. I myself have never applied for parole and never shall, which is why I can afford the luxury of veracity and free expression.

SECTIONS 3 & 4 OF THE LETTER ARE REMOVED

(5) Myra's apparent offer to undergo hypnosis to aid recollection. When I advised that it should be drug-induced hypnosis (Sodium Pentothal, which corrodes subconscious defence mechanisms), she dropped the idea.

SECTION 6 OF THE LETTER IS REMOVED

Add to this the published fact that, (a) her seven years of coded letters are in the hands of my solicitors, (b) an autobiography I wrote many years ago lies in a vault and is to be released after my death or until I instruct otherwise.

In the aforementioned Panorama programme, former Home Office Minister A. Widdicombe stated there are twenty-three prisoners in the UK who will never be released. Why has the public heard so little of them? In this and other special hospitals run by prison warders there are also patients no-one has heard of, who have been rotting behind bars for forty and fifty years for relatively minor offences. That puts the present loud debate over Myra Hindley in proper perspective, and crystallises the reason why I have long advocated UK prisoners and patients in special hospitals should have access to voluntary euthanasia.

I would wish this statement to be published in full, no matters raised being taken out of proper context, distorted or sensationalised.

Yours faithfully,

Ian Brady

In 1998, when she was launching yet another appeal against her sentence, Myra admitted that Ian knew that he had kept the letters and that they would be very damaging to her case. Her appeal rested on the claim that Ian had forced her to participate in the murders. Now she was desperately afraid that he would release the letters as he had mentioned they had corresponded in his 1997 letter to Jack Straw.

In an interview with The Telegraph and a letter to the telegraph Myra claims that she was threatened by Brady into committing the murders and that she would release photographs showing the extent of the abuse suffered at the hands of Brady.

"When the abuse and duress and very probably those photographs are used at my appeal, Brady will be enraged,"

said Hindley.

"And no doubt [he] will instruct Birnberg to reveal that and all the other messages from my letters to him."

In the interview Myra admits that the letters would not show her in a good light, but claims that again she was coerced into producing them by the power of Ian Brady.

In the event, Ian didn't even have to release the letters. Myra had never been going to get off. After her appeal failed Ian scoffed at her immense stupidity in mentioning them at all, let alone referring to their secret code.

She shot herself in the foot,

he wrote,

by mentioning them and the coded methodology. As for the suggestion I told her to write certain messages, that too was an error and a vast underestimation of general intelligence and credulity.

Catch 22. She had to invent some excuse and, in the circumstances, she had no real choice

Of course, even after their relationship had come to an end, neither Myra nor Ian stopped writing letters. For Myra in particular, letters were her link to the outside world. It was a way of staying in contact with her family, all of whom she appears to have still loved very much – even Maureen, who had shopped her to the police, together with her husband David.

In the early years, Myra often wrote to her grandmother about how much she missed Ian – often referring to him as "Neddie, which was one of her pet names for him. However, when their relationship had soured, Myra's correspondents mostly read about her yearning to be free and her various appeals for parole.

Both Myra and Ian carried on correspondences with members of the media. For Myra, it was a way of trying to garner support for her bids for freedom. Ian, on the other hand, mostly used it in his attempt to "get even" with Myra and, perhaps, to enjoy the attention he received as the male half of Britain's most notorious serial killers.

He was obsessed with Peter Topping, who was the Detective Chief Superintendent who oversaw the investigation into the disappearance of Pauline Reade and that of Keith Bennett, and often wrote about him to Brendan Pittaway, a journalist with whom he was in contact for a number of years up to the early 1990s. To Brendan, he claimed that he and Myra had both agreed to stop writing to each other, although the truth was that he had been very much dumped by her. Ian also revealed his paranoia; he always signed his envelopes on the seal so that he would know whether or not they'd been opened, and expressed his outrage when Topping made money from an interview he carried out twenty-five years after Myra and Ian had been arrested.

Myra stopped at nothing in her ever-more desperate attempts to be released from prison. The family of Lesley Ann Downey had been deeply involved in campaigning against Myra's release from jail ever since the idea of Myra eventually qualifying from parole had been mooted. The fact that Myra had been increasingly disassociated with reality was revealed when she actually wrote to Lesley Ann's mother in an attempt to persuade her to call off her campaign. She wrote of how she had changed, saying that she was "not what I was all those years ago" and mentioned how upset she was whenever she was referred to as "evil."

Myra wrote:

"You couldn't hate me more than I hate myself. I have asked God for His forgiveness, but I couldn't ask for yours, for how can I ever expect you to forgive me when I cannot forgive myself. I know almost everyone

describes me as cold and calculating – 'evil Myra' – but I ask you to believe that I find all this deeply upsetting."

Despite the ample evidence to the contrary, in the form of the pornographic images that Myra and Ian had taken of little Lesley Ann, and Myra's harsh words to her, captured forever on tape, Myra insisted to the child's mother that the little girl had not been tortured.

In 1986, Keith Bennett's mother Winnie wrote to Myra, begging her to reveal all she knew about where Keith was buried. Myra answered, saying only that she didn't know where Ian had buried the child, not wishing to be seen to be involved.

Winnie's desperate plea as a letter to Myra Hindley was as follows:

Dear Miss Hindley,

I am sure I am one of the last people you would ever expected to receive a letter from. I am the mother of Keith Bennett who went missing, no-one knows where, on June 16, 1964. As a woman I am sure you can envisage the nightmare I have lived with day and night, 24 hours a day, since then. Not knowing whether my son is alive or dead, whether he ran away or was taken away, is literally a living hell, something which you no doubt have experienced during your many, many years locked in prison.

My letter to you is written out of desperation and faint hope, desperation because I know that for so many years neither you nor Ian Brady has ever admitted knowing anything about my son's disappearance, and hope that Christianity has softened your soul so much that you would never any longer knowingly condemn someone to permanent purgatory. Please I beg of you, tell me what happened to Keith. My heart tells me you know and I am on bended knees begging you to end this torture and finally put my mind at rest. Besides asking for your pity, the only other thing I can say is that by helping me you will doubtless help yourself because those people who have harboured so much hate against you and prevented your being released a long time ago would have no reason left to harbour their hate. By telling me what happened to Keith you would be announcing loudly to the world that you really have turned into the kind, caring, warm person that Lord Longford speaks of.

I am a simple woman, I work in the kitchens of Christie's Hospital, it has taken me five weeks labour to write this letter because it is so important to me that it is understood by you for what it is, a plea for help.

Please Miss Hindley help me.

Mrs W. Johnson.

Later, after yet another failed attempt to secure her release from prison, Myra wrote:

"I have written to the Home Office and the Parole Board to say I do not wish to be considered for parole in 1990, and my own belief is that I shall probably remain in prison until I die."

However, perhaps the bulk of Myra's prison correspondence was to and from the men who supported her improbable bids for freedom, Lord Longford and Observer editor David Astor. Myra's letters suggest that she had a closer relationship with David Astor. In 1985 she wrote to him:

"If the road to hell is paved with good intentions, I have a very long, well-paved private road."

Myra's letters must have convinced Astor that she was not only redeemable, but redeemed. In 1989, seven years before her death, he wrote to her:

"As you know, the more you show yourself to be both normal and intelligent, the more people will want to know how anyone like that could have lived on [another] level. Until you can somehow find a convincing way of describing that, people will be puzzled and confused."

Myra also corresponded with Duncan Staff, a contributor to The Guardian newspaper. Although Lord Longford had been her stalwart supporter since 1968, she had grown tired of him and had realised that many of his attempts to help her campaign actually backfired. She wrote to Duncan Staff that:

"Frank has been a pestilential pain in the neck over the years with his 'campaigning' and he glories in the publicity himself. God help me; he wrote an article a couple of months ago which was published in the Catholic Herald, and was over the moon because they offered him a column once a month where, he said, he can write whatever he wants about me to

promote my cause. God knows I've caused so much suffering in my life, but this is a cross that I can well do without!"

In 1994 came the killer letter to Myra from the Head of the Tarif unit for UK sentencing informing Miss Hindley that her appeals would no longer be heard by the Parole Board and that it would from now on be the decision of Government Ministers. This letter would have been a blow to Myra who would be under no doubt that she would spend the rest of her days incarcerated.

Miss M Hindley

HM Prison Cookham Wood

Dear Miss Hindley,

In accordance with the House of Lords' judgment of 24 June 1993 in Doody and others, I am writing to inform you of the substance of the judicial recommendations which were made in your case as to the period to be served by you in order to satisfy the requirements of retribution and deterrence (the tariff), together with the decision of the Secretary of State of the day in July 1990 as to the appropriate period in question. I should emphasise that this is disclosure of the judicial recommendations, and of the decision taken by previous Ministers.

Although your solicitor made representations on your behalf on 5 December, and invited the Secretary of State to reduce the tariff before the material contained in this letter had been disclosed, it is considered inappropriate for the Secretary of State to reconsider the matter until you have had the opportunity to make full representations in response to the disclosures made in this letter. The Secretary of State will then consider your tariff afresh.

Following your conviction, the trial judge wrote to the Secretary of State on 8 May 1966. He explained that he had not made a recommendation in passing sentence, because the only possible one at that stage would have been that you should never be set free again. He hoped that, apart from some dramatic conversion, you would be kept in prison for a very long time. He did not suggest any term of years. A full copy of his letter is enclosed.

The then Lord Chief Justice, Lord Widgery, was consulted in 1978. He replied in March 1978: "... I do not think that we can usefully discuss what the ultimate term of imprisonment might be." A full copy of his letter is enclosed.

In January 1982, the Lord Chief Justice (then Lord Jane) was consulted about the appropriate period of detention. He said that he did "not think that any term less than 25 years would be appropriate in the circumstances". A full copy of his letter of 12 January 1982 is enclosed.

In January 1985, the Lord Chief Justice (Lord Lane) was consulted again (the trial judge having died). The Lord Chief Justice referred back to his letter of 12 January 1982 and added: "I should emphasise that the suggested period of 25 years in Hindley's case was indeed a minimum." A copy of the standard consultation proforma and Lord Lane's letter of 10 January 1985 is enclosed, together with copies of the papers attached to it.

At that stage, Ministers decided to set a 30-year tariff in your case which, however, they described as "provisional".

In July 1990, Ministers again reviewed the question of what your tariff should be. They were then aware of your confession to the police in February 1987, but took it into account only in so far as it shed light on the circumstances of the offences for which you were sentenced to life imprisonment for murder. The Secretary of State of the day (Lord Waddington) concluded on 26 July 1990 that a whole life tariff should be imposed in your case. He did so taking into account the circumstances of the offences in question having regard to the other comparable cases.

As he indicated in the statement of 27 July 1993, the Secretary of State is willing to consider any written representations by prisoners as to the period to be served by them to satisfy the requirements of retribution and deterrence.

If, therefore, you, or those acting on your behalf, wish to make further written representations in connection with the matters set out in this letter, the Secretary of State will give them careful consideration, together with the representations submitted by your solicitor on 5 December 1994.

On 7 December 1994, the Secretary of State announced that new review arrangements would apply to life sentence prisoners (a copy of the announcement is attached).

Under these new arrangements, life sentence prisoners with whole life tariffs will no longer have their cases reviewed by the Parole Board, except where such a review has already been fixed (in your case the Parole Board review scheduled for August 1995 will go ahead). In future, life sentences prisoners with whole life tariffs will have their cases reviewed only by Ministers, who will consider whether or not the whole life tariff remains appropriate.

These reviews will take place at the 10-year and 25-year points in the sentence, and, where appropriate, every 5 years thereafter, as described in the announcement.

Yours sincerely, I A Newton Head of Tariff Unit

As time passed and the parents of Myra and Ian's victims grew older, the matter of finding the graves of the victims who had never been discovered became increasingly pressing. Winnie Johnston, Keith Bennett's mother, even wrote to Myra to beg for her help in finding the little boy's grave so that he could finally be laid to rest and given a Christian burial. There was a feeling that if there was any hope that one of the Moors Murderers would repent and reveal their victims' final resting place, Myra would be the one. But despite Myra's apparent attempts to help, her secrets accompanied her to the grave – or more accurately, the crematorium – when she died in 2002 aged 60.

Although child molesters typically have a very difficult time in prison and often have to be isolated from the rest of the prisoners for their own safety, for some reason Ian was largely left alone and he formed friendships with some of Britain's most notorious criminals, including Peter Sutcliffe (known better as the 'Yorkshire Ripper') and Ronnie Kray.

By 2006, Ian had very much given up on life. He had gone on hunger strike and was force-fed every day to keep him alive. He compared himself to Argentina's General Pinochet (then facing trial for crimes against his people, which he eventually evaded because he was not strong enough), saying,

"And now I sit chained to a drip feed every morning at 5.30, getting my legal and social correspondence done, reminiscing."

That year, he wrote to Keith Bennett's mother for the first time but, rather than bringing her the welcome news of where the little boy was buried, he devoted most of his letter to moaning about being force fed and the conditions in the jail where he was being held.

All Ian wanted, according to his own testimony, was to die.

In 2012, there was a startling development in Ian's case when his mental health advocate was arrested as part of a criminal investigation. It turned out that the police were looking into the possibility that Ian had written a letter, intended to be sent to Keith Bennett's mother after his death, that revealed the location of Keith's grave. According to Jackie Powell, the advocate, he had written the letter and told her about it, had even shown to her. When she was asked why she had not revealed the letter to the police, she commented only that her duty of care was to Ian Brady and not to anyone else. Powell was duly arrested and held in custody while the police searched her home and Ian's cell for any trace of the letter. No such letter was found. The fact that Keith's mother had died shortly before the search only served to add to the pathos and tragedy of the situation.

Picture Credits

All interior images are courtesy of Rex Features

Cover Credits

(tl) Bettmann/Corbis, (tr) Kovnir Andrii/Shutterstock, ChameleonsEye/
Shutterstock, (bc) Bettmann/Corbis, (b) J. Wilds/Hulton Archive/Getty Images